The Magic 'Degh'

SIKH STORIES FOR CHILDREN

The Magic 'Degh'

SIKH STORIES FOR CHILDREN

UNIVERSAL VALUES FROM SIKH LEGENDS & TRADITIONS

NARRATOR
PUSHPENDRA SINGH

KW
KW Publishers Pvt Ltd
New Delhi

KVW

KW Publishers Pvt Ltd
4676/21, First Floor, Ansari Road, Daryaganj, New Delhi 110002
E mail@kwpub.in/knowledgeworld@vsnl.net T +91.11.23263498 / 43528107
w w w . k w p u b . i n

ISBN 978-93-80502-63-2

Published by Kalpana Shukla, KW Publishers Pvt Ltd
4676/21, First Floor, Ansari Road, Daryaganj, New Delhi 110002

Cover and text illustrations by Ms Kanwal Bir

Printed and bound in India

Dedicated to

My Parents,
Narindar Kartar Singh,
& Maj-General Kartar Singh, PVSM
from whom I first heard the *Saakhis*

❧

For

Our grandchildren,
Jaanvi, Jaiditya & Aarav

❧

Contents

1. The Sikhs: Legends and Traditions 1
2. The Child Nanak 6
3. The Sacred Thread 10
4. Three Golden Rules 13
5. We are all Brothers 17
6. The Sweet Taste of Truth and Honesty 23
7. Guru Nanak at Haridwar 29
8. The Multi-crorepati 33
9. Where is God? 37
10. The Faqir of Hasan Abdal 41
11. Babur Conquers Punjab 46
12. The Guru's Langar 51
13. Guru-Sahib and Humayun 54
14. Shelter for the Homeless 60
15. The Greedy Merchant 63
16. The Emperor and the Magical Degh 68
17. Baba Buddha-Ji 73
18. The Durbar Sahib 77
19. Jahangir 81
20. Miri–Piri Da Malik 86

21. Painde Khan   94

22. Guru Har Rai—The Seventh Guru   98

23. The Saviour from Suffering   102

24. Guru Tegh Bahadur Ji   110

25. Guru Tegh Bahadur's Personal Example   114

26. Guru Gobind and Syed Budhu Shah   123

27. Creation of the Khalsa   129

28. The Charm of the Khalsa   138

29. Anandpur Besieged   146

30. A Horrible Crime   154

31. Forgiveness for the Traitors   160

32. An Eternal Guru   163

33. Banda Bahadur—The First Sikh Ruler   170

34. Magic of the 'Degh' in Modern Times   175.

Acknowledgements

Dr. Gurpal S Bhuller is a renowned orthopaedic surgeon from USA and a very well read Sikh. He is the author of a delightful book, 'The Enquiring Guru – Questions by the Sikh Gurus and their Answers'. This provides perceptive insights into the Gurbani. Besides his very busy medical practice, he is deeply involved in philanthropic projects in India, Malaysia and USA. Yet when I asked him if he would care to go through the manuscript of this compilation, he readily agreed. Despite his heavy commitments, he did a most thorough job, made many valuable suggestions, pointed out numerous inaccuracies and went through the text most meticulously.

My father, Maj Gen Kartar Singh, despite being over 90, also went through the manuscript and made suggestions which are all the more valuable, as he and my mother had first recounted to me most of these legends as a child. My wife, Kanwal Bir – Jotan, as she is better known – was also deeply involved in our endeavour from its inception and she has illustrated the *saakhis* and done the cover painting with loving dedication.

My Granddaughter Jaanvi, is an avid reader. She went through most of the chapters and pointed out the words or phrases which could be difficult for a 10-year old to understand. My niece, Jotika Cartwright, eagerly went through the manuscript text and suggested many improvements in the short time she had during a lightning visit.

Despite making every effort to maintain authenticity and accuracy of the legends, I am alone responsible for any factual errors that may still remain.

'*Truth is One, but Sages speak of it by many names.*'

— The Rig Veda

1

The Sikhs: Legends and Traditions

As a little girl, Jaanvi, my first grandchild, loved listening to stories. So, I would read her stories like Snow White, Cinderella, and other fairy tales. Once, while we were sharing these stories, she asked me, 'Naanoo, is Guru Nanak God?'

'No, sweet heart, he was a Teacher who explained how we all could be better human beings.'

'Then who is God?'

'God is the one who created all of us and the whole universe.' Her little brother, Jaiditya piped in, 'Naanoo, God *hum sab ko maar sakte hain?*'

'No, *beta*, God loves us all and He doesn't hurt anyone.'

Then, Jaanvi, '*Sab religions ke* God *alag alag kyon hotay hain?*'

'No, Jaanvi. God created all human beings, and also all animals and plants. In fact, everything. He is the same for everyone and everything'. Both children became quiet for a few minutes, thinking this over—perhaps revising their earlier ideas.

Then, 'Naanoo, who are Sikhs?'

To answer her question I started telling the children some Saakhis of Guru Nanak and other Gurus, which my parents used to tell us. This book is an attempt at re-telling some Saakhis and other true episodes which illustrate the core values and main traditions of the Sikhs. But to answer Jaanvi's question....

Guru Nanak Dev Ji

Who Are Sikhs?

The Sikh religion was founded by Guru Nanak who first spelt out certain core values. These universal ideals are at the heart of the Sikh faith. Guru Nanak's principles are for all mankind, not just for Sikhs. More than two hundred years later, Guru Nanak's fundamental belief— all men are created equal—was echoed by Thomas Jefferson in the American Declaration of Independence in 1776.

President Thomas Jefferson of USA

Guru Nanak, the first Guru lived nearly 550 years ago (1469–1539 AD). At that time the people of Hindustan were divided mainly into Hindus and Muslims. Hindu people were also split into four castes and worshipped many forms of God. They married only within their own religion and caste. Higher caste Hindus regarded the ones from the lower castes as unclean. They kept separate utensils for giving them water or food and would not eat in their homes.

Guru Nanak firmly believed that there is only 'One Creator', who has created the Universe and everything in it—living or non-living. This Creator loves everyone; hates no one and has no fear. He has always existed and will be there for ever—He is the Eternal Being or *Akaal Purakh*.

Therefore, he believed that all people in the world

have been created equal and we should be gentle and caring towards all human beings—in fact, by helping fellow beings one can experience God. Men and women are also equal. He hated treating some human beings as lower than others. Further he said that we should live and work honestly and share what we earn, with others. To help us do these things we should always keep God's name in our minds.

Six centuries ago, at the time of Guru Nanak, women did not have the same position as men. Hence, the idea that men and women are equal was radical. In fact, four hundred years after Guru Nanak first said that women and men are equal, there was a strong movement in United Kingdom and America to give women the same rights as men. It took many years for the Governments of these two most advanced nations of that time to grant equality to women. So, Guru Nanak's views were very modern and remain important in the 21st Century.

Before he died, Guru Nanak named one of his disciples, *Bhai* (Brother) Lehna as the next one to continue with his teachings. Each Guru then named the next Teacher to follow him until Guru Gobind Singh, the tenth Guru (1666–1708). By this time all the teachings in the form of hymns, had been compiled in a book or *granth*. Guru Gobind Singh then said that there would be no living Guru after him but the *Granth Sahib* should be regarded as the Guru after his death.

Now we can answer the question 'Who is a Sikh?' A Sikh essentially believes in the One, Eternal Creator and follows the teachings of the ten Gurus and Guru Granth Sahib.

This book re-tells some legends from the life of Guru Nanak and from those of nine Gurus who followed him. The episodes have been selected from Sikh history. They recount personal examples given by the Gurus and others about the ideals of Sikhism and all of humanity.

🍷 🍷

2

The Child Nanak

Guru Nanak was born in 1469 at Talwandi near Lahore, which is now in Pakistan. North India was then ruled by Muslim invaders and Talwandi, as well as the area around it, was owned by a Muslim landlord, Rai Bular. Guru Nanak's sister, Nanki, was five years older than him. Their father, Mehta Kalu, worked for Rai Bular as his *patwari* or estate-manager. Rai Bular was a good man and treated the Hindu people under him kindly. Mehta Kalu worked very sincerely and that was the reason why Rai Bular liked and respected him. Later, when Nanak grew a little older, he also became very fond of the young boy.

Nanak played lots of games with friends of his age in Talwandi. However, he specially liked to gather his friends at a cool, grassy place near a pond. There he would ask them to join in singing with him and soon Nanak and his friends would be singing joyfully. Most often Nanak sang a hymn *'Dhan Nirankar; Sat Kartar.'* This means 'Praise the True Creator, who has no form.' Nanak sang from his heart which was so filled with deep love for God that it touched everyone's heart and gave them a lot of joy.

Joyful children

One day Rai Bular was passing close to this spot. When he heard the sounds of children singing happily and joyfully he asked his companion, 'Who are these children?'

'*Huzoor* that one, who is leading the group is Nanak; *patwari* sahib's son. The others are his friends.'

'Let's stop for a while—I somehow find the sounds of such cheerful singing so pleasing to the ears.'

'And to the heart too, *huzoor?*' Rai Bular nodded in agreement as he moved closer to the children. When they approached the group they found many passers-by also standing there, charmed by the singing. Some had even joined in and were clapping softly to the beat.

Watching Nanak, an image flashed before Rai Bular's eyes. He turned to his companion, 'I saw Nanak the other day fast asleep while his cattle were grazing. The shadow of the tree had moved away from him, but I saw a cobra with its hood open next to the child.'

'Was he bitten by the snake?'

'I had thought so too; so I picked up a stick and went to chase it away. But the snake glided away. Apparently, he had been shading Nanak's face.'

'I saw a cobra shading Nanak!'

'*Wallah!* He is no ordinary child. I tell you, he will bring great renown to our village.'

His words were prophetic for Nanak grew up to become

the Divine Teacher, or Guru. Rai Bular then had a room built at the spot near the pond, which he converted into a permanent tank for storing water.

When he turned six, Guru Nanak was sent to school. He loved learning to read, write, and do arithmetic, which were the subjects taught in those days. He was a gifted student and in just a few years he knew everything that the teacher could teach him.

Thus, from early childhood, Guru Nanak's love for God and very high intelligence revealed that he was no ordinary person, but a Divine Being.

3

The Sacred Thread

Nanak was excited and happy because it was his ninth birthday. But instead of wearing new clothes and, despite the morning chill, his upper body was bare and he was dressed waist down, in a *tehmat*—a plain, ankle-length cloth wrapped around his waist. Patiently, his mother explained that today he would put on the sacred thread or *janeu*. The family priest had been asked to come and do the religious ceremonies. Best of all, there would be a feast afterwards since many friends and neighbours had been invited to the ceremony along with the family. Obediently he sat down next to the *havan* or sacred fire, as indicated by his mother, but questions kept popping up in Nanak's mind. Why should I wear this thread? What good will it do for me? He decided to ask the priest. Folding his hands respectfully he asked, '*Panditji* why are you putting this cotton thread on me?'

The priest had never before been asked this question, but he smiled kindly and answered, 'This is a sacred thread and for thousands of years Hindu boys and men of higher caste wear it. This *janeu* will make you a better person and you can enter heaven only if you wear it.'

'Panditji, why should I wear this thread?'

Guru Nanak was not satisfied with this answer and thought about it for some minutes. Then he told the priest, 'There is nothing to stop anyone from wearing a cotton thread. Even bad men who rob and kill people can wear it. I think it is more important to speak the truth, be kind to others, do good deeds, and have no evil thoughts. Surely these are the things which will make one a better person, fit to go to heaven.'

There was a buzz of amazement from neighbours and friends of Nanak's parents who had come to witness the thread ceremony. Someone said out loud what everyone was thinking, 'This is no ordinary child. He will become a great man and make Talwandi a famous place.'

Nanak did not wear the *janeu*; he did not believe in blind rituals.

The person who spoke out everyone's thoughts was so prophetic. Nanak became a Divine Teacher whose teaching attracted millions of people, even kings and emperors. Talwandi is now called Nankana Sahib and people from all over the world come in thousands just to be at the place where such a great person was born and lived—and to pray at the Gurudwara there. Even when he had grown up Guru Nanak remembered this incident and put his ideas about the *janeu* in a verse forming part of the prayer called 'Asa di Vaar'.

4

Three Golden Rules

Guru Nanak and his elder sister, Nanki were very fond of each other. She grew up, married and went to live with her husband, Diwan Jai Ram who worked for the Governor of Sultanpur. When Guru Nanak became a young man, Jai Ram was able to find a job for him as in-charge of Governor Daulat Khan's *modikhana* or store house. This was where the tax that the land-owners and others gave was stored. In those days the tax was paid partly out of the foodstuffs which the villagers grew in the fields. So the storehouse was full of wheat, rice, *gur*, cotton and other dry produce. All of this was stored properly, weighed and kept in the *modikhana*.

Some of these items were given out as part of the salary of the Government employees such as police and Army; some went to Nawab Daulat Khan's house, while the remaining items were sold to the people. A record of all the items with their weights, either coming in to the *modikhana* or being paid out from it, was carefully kept. An account of the money received was also kept and the cash deposited in the Governor's treasury. Guru Nanak was going to be the new *modi*, in charge of the stores and their correct records.

Every morning Nanak would wake up about three hours before sunrise and go to the Bein River for a bath. Then he would sit on its banks and let his mind dwell on the Creator. Filled with bliss, he would sing songs celebrating His wonders. Only after this would he go for his work.

As always, Guru Nanak performed his duties extremely well and with total honesty. While he worked, he thought about the miracle of creation—cool water in the streams; leafy trees and green fields; the liquid calls of the *bulbul* birds and so on. His heart sang with joy about the marvels of *Akaal Purakh* and an expression of delight came over his face. When people came to him for any work, they could not help but be touched by his happiness and in turn, they too felt uplifted. He treated everyone with great courtesy and had a smile and kind words for all. He was very fair in charging the right amount and giving every one the correct measure of goods. The Guru was specially gentle towards poor people and often gave away things from his own rations to the needy. Because of this, the people and the Nawab's servants grew to love and honour him.

While Guru Nanak was counting out the measures he was giving out, his mind would focus on *Akaal Purakh*. Often when he came to the number thirteen, *tayraan* in Punjabi, he would silently think, 'All the foodstuffs in the storehouse are actually Yours, (i.e., God's creation)'.

In Punjabi, yours is *tayrah*. He would then continue to count out *tayrah*, *tayrah* ... and often give away much more than the required number of measures to poor people.

He was specially gentle towards poor people

However, some persons did not like Nanak becoming so popular. Maybe they did not receive extra favours which they might have got earlier. They made a false complaint to the Nawab saying, 'Your *modi* does not keep his mind on his work; he is very careless and dishonest and gives away huge amounts to his friends. Soon your *modikhana* will be empty and then the *modi* will run away.'

The Nawab was very upset on hearing this complaint and got his store and accounts thoroughly checked. However, everything was found to be absolutely correct.

Nawab Daulat Khan praised Guru Nanak's work and also put to shame the persons who had made the false complaint.

After this incident people began to love Guru Nanak even more than before. Even Daulat Khan gave him a lot of respect. People began to ask him the secret of his happiness. Guru Nanak told them that he followed three rules and if they wanted to be happy they should also do the same:-

First, he said, 'Earn your living with honest work and never be idle.' Second, 'Share your earnings with others; help weaker people, give food to the hungry and clothes to those who cannot afford them.'

Third, he said, 'Always remember *Akaal Purakh*.' If you follow these golden rules, you will be truly contented.

In Punjabi these golden rules are known as: '*Kirat karo; vand chhakko; Naam japo.*'

☞☜

5

We are all Brothers

After working for about twelve years with Nawab Daulat Khan, Guru Nanak began to feel the urge and longing to serve *Sat-Kartar* and His children. So, despite Daulat Khan's pleading, he decided to leave and live among the common and poor people. After clearing the *modikhana* accounts and stores he received the salary which was due to him. This, along with all his personal possessions, he gave away to poor and needy people.

He put on saffron clothes like holy men of that time, who have given up worldly things, bid goodbye to his wife, family members and friends and went into the countryside outside the town of Sultanpur. There he sat under a shady jujube berry *(ber)* tree and meditated in silence on *Akaal Purakh*. Many people were drawn to him and sat quietly next to his holy presence. He would bathe in the Bein River every morning before dawn and start his meditation before sunrise. After that he would talk to the small crowd of devotees who waited patiently every day to listen to him and would hang onto every word that he said.

River Bein

One day the devotees arrived at sunrise just like before, but Guru-Ji was not to be seen. They got alarmed when they found his clothes neatly piled up near the *Beri*, as if he had just gone for his usual bath in the river. When he did not return till late in the day, they organised search parties to look for Guru-Ji up and down the river. For three days and nights there was no sign of him. Then the next morning the devotees found him sitting under the *Beri* as usual. One of the devotees observed that there seemed to be a glow coming from him. He quietly remarked about it to his companion. Soon a whispered buzz went around about the radiance coming from the Guru's person. After a while Guru-Ji came out from his deep meditation and his presence filled all his devotees with a calm happiness. Then he broke his silence and said, 'There is no Hindu and no Musalmaan.'

In Punjab those days, people were either Hindu or Muslim (Musalmaan). Punjab was also under the rule of Muslims who had invaded the land and defeated the Hindu rulers about 400 years ago. Although the rulers of this period did not force Hindus to become Muslims; but they also did not tolerate anyone attracting Muslims to any other religion. Hence, Guru Nanak's message was quite revolutionary and soon, everyone was repeating with astonishment what he had said. When the Nawab's *Qazi* or magistrate, heard this he complained angrily to Daulat Khan, who summoned Guru Nanak to his court.

The Guru obeyed the Nawab's order and went to his court. Daulat Khan seated him by his side, saying to the *Qazi*, 'Put your questions to him.'

The *Qazi* asked Guru Nanak, 'How can you say that there are no Hindus and no Musalmans? There are hundreds of Muslims in this very town and many thousands more in the Sultanate.'

Guru Nanak replied, 'It is true that thousands of people call themselves Muslim and thousands more say they are Hindu. But truly there are no Hindus and no Musalamans.'

Guru-Ji observed that the Nawab and *Qazi* were listening intently to him. He went on, 'Both Muslims and Hindus have forgotten the basics of their religions. All Muslims and Hindus have been created by the Creator. In fact all human beings have been created equal but we ourselves have raised artificial walls between each other.' Now the Nawab and the *Qazi* shook their heads in agreement and became even more thoughtful as they reflected on the Guru's words.

'True Hindus or true Muslims should only do what pleases *Sat-Kartar*: show kindness to all and harm no one. Never be arrogant or greedy and never rob what belongs to others; always be truthful and humble.'

Then he repeated his golden rules: *Kirat karo; Vand chhakko; Naam japo.*

He turned his attention to the *Qazi*, '*Qazi*, sahib please look around you and tell me how many people can truly call themselves Hindu or Muslim. That is why I said that there is no Hindu and no Musalmaan.'

The *Qazi* had no answer while the Nawab respectfully folded his hands, bowed and said, 'You are absolutely correct! It appears as if God has spoken through you. I will certainly try to become a true Musalmaan.'

As Guru Nanak got up to leave, they heard the muezzin's call for the afternoon *namaaz*—the Muslim prayers. At once the Nawab looked towards the Guru and said, 'You have declared that Muslims and Hindus are children of the same God. Since we are going for *namaaz*, will you join us in prayer to our common Father?

Guru Nanak agreed at once and went with them to the mosque. The *Qazi* stood up and began the *namaaz* and the worshippers joined him. However, the Guru remained seated in respectful silence. After the *namaaz* the Nawab reproached him, 'You had promised to join us in the *namaaz* but you did not do so.'

The Guru replied, 'It is true I promised to join you in prayer but you were actually somewhere else, so how could I join you?'

'No, I was here before your eyes and saying the prayers aloud.'

'Yes your body was indeed here, reciting the words of prayer, but your mind was actually in Kabul, where you were buying horses.'

'You were actually in Kabul buying horses!'

Daulat Khan was surprised that Guru-Ji had found out what he was actually thinking while he seemed to be praying. He bowed before the Guru, 'Yes, you are right! I really was thinking about the horses, which I had sent my men to buy in Kabul. But our *Qazi* is deeply religious. Surely, he would have said his prayers with a true heart, so you could have joined him.'

Guru Nanak replied, 'No, unfortunately the *Qazi* was thinking about the new-born foal at home. He had forgotten to tell his servants to tie it properly and was worried that it would fall into the well in his compound.'

Now it was the *Qazi* who bowed before the Guru, 'You are absolutely right, O man of God, we must indeed pray with our full mind and heart.'

'Yes,' said the Guru, 'God hears our prayers when said with a pure heart.'

6

The Sweet Taste of Truth and Honesty

Soon after he showed Nawab Daulat Khan and the *Qazi* how to become good Musalmaans Guru Nanak left Sultanpur and began travelling around the country to spread his message across to more and more people. He had put his teachings into simple hymns or *shabads* and he took along with him Bhai Mardana, a poor Muslim minstrel with a charming voice, who accompanied him while playing a guitar-like instrument called *rabaab*. Mardana loved the *shabads* and sang them from his heart. Presently, they came to Eminabad, a town near Gujranwala, now in Pakistan.

Going straight to the locality area where poor people lived, Guru Nanak stopped before a small hut. Mardana remarked, 'It has been kept very neat and clean and is free from litter.'

'Yes,' agreed Guru Nanak, 'looks like the owner is still hard at working. He also appears to be an honest fellow; maybe we can stay with him for a few days, if he will keep us'

Lalo, a poor carpenter, looked up from his work bench

and saw two strangers standing outside his humble hut. He resumed work but immediately looked up again, attracted by the goodness glowing in Guru Nanak. He dusted off his hands and clothes and hurried to welcome them into his home with folded hands.

Guru Nanak and Mardana at Lalo's house

Hindu society was divided into four castes depending to which parents one was born. All high-caste *brahmins* (priests) and *khatris* (warriors) used to avoid even touching people whom they believed were of low-caste and never had anything to eat or drink from them. They even did the same with Muslims. So a high-caste *khatri* like Guru Nanak, travelling with a Muslim and entering the house of a lowly carpenter was really a very bold step.

Lalo made the Guru comfortable on a charpoy and asked Mardana to sit on a mat, since there was no chair or other furniture piece in the one-roomed hut. He then went to the well and hauled up some cool, fresh water for them to drink and wash up. After this, he sat cross-legged on the floor and began cooking a simple meal for his guests.

When he served the coarse, dry *roti* and *saag* to them, Bhai Mardana hesitated to eat such taste-less looking food and glanced uncertainly towards the Guru. But Guru Nanak had already begun to relish the food. Bhai Mardana found the food to be surprisingly tasty and exclaimed, 'This meal is really delicious! What *masala* have you used to cook it?'

Guru Nanak smiled at Mardana, 'It has the sweet flavour of truthfulness and honesty!'

Though a very poor man, Lalo did not hesitate to share food with his guests. In fact, he actually practised Guru Nanak's three golden rules. The Guru was very fond of good and kind people like Lalo and he embraced him to his heart.

While staying in Lalo's hut, Bhai Mardana and Guru Nanak would go every morning to the outskirts of the town, sit under a shady tree to pray and meditate on the *Akaal Purakh*. Mardana would then play the *rabaab* and sing the Guru's *shabads*. Attracted by the sweet music, people gathered around the Guru in large numbers. He explained the *shabads* to the people, which conveyed his simple ideas. 'We have all been made by *Sat-Kartar*, hence, there are no Hindus or Musalmaans; all human beings have been created equal.' He went on to explain his three golden rules and everyone was struck by the sincerity and truth in his words. Lalo and many many more of the townspeople began to adore the Guru and became his Sikhs.

At the same time, a buzz went around the town that this high-caste, holy man was actually living in Lalo's house. Some rich and high-caste Hindus did not like the Guru doing these things, which they thought were against their religion. So they went to take Guru-Ji from Lalo's hut and waited outside it to meet him. 'Holy sir,' they said, 'you are moving with a Muslim companion and staying in a low-caste man's dirty hut. Such actions are not proper for a high-caste Hindu and violate our religious code.'

Ignoring their comment of the 'dirty hut' because though poor, it was in fact very clean and tidy, Guru-Ji replied 'I am not Hindu or Muslim and neither do I belong to any caste;' adding, 'like all of us, I too have been created by God. So, the only religion I follow is to serve my fellow beings.' The rich people were unable to persuade Guru-Ji to come away with them and soon left.

One day Malik Bhago, a high government officer, gave a feast for the high-caste townsfolk and also invited Guru Nanak.

'Holy sir,' Malik Bhago said, 'you are staying in the house of a low-caste carpenter and eating dry *rotis*. This is not correct for a high-born *khatri*. Please come for my feast and share the most delicious dishes that are being prepared.'

But Guru-Ji did not want to go and told him, 'I am a simple *faqir* (a hermit) and I find this plain food quite enough for my needs.'

On Malik's insistence and entreaties, Guru Nanak went with him for the feast but he did not eat any food. Malik Bhago asked him impatiently, 'There is delicious food here; why do you refuse to eat it?'

In answer Guru-Ji took out a dry *roti* which he had brought from Bhai Lalo's house and held it in his right hand. Then he picked up a *parantha* (pancake) dripping with butter, in his left. He said, 'See, here in my right hand I hold a roti made by Lalo.' He extended his right hand. 'Now in my left hand, I hold a *parantha* from your feast.' He extended the left hand with the *parantha*.

'Now I squeeze both the *rotis*.' He observed the other guests listening to him with rapt attention and watching the squeezing motion of his hands. 'What would come out of Lalo's *roti*?' he asked one of them.

The man saw white fluid dripping from that hand and answered, 'Milk!'

'And from the other?' Guru-Ji inquired from another guest.

Without thinking the man blurted out what popped unexpectedly into his mind. 'Sire, blood!' — as if he had really seen blood dripping from Guru-Ji's left hand.

Guru-Sahib was pleased with the answers given by both people.

'See, Malik Bhago, money made by taking advantage of poor, innocent people is like sucking their blood. How can I eat a *parantha* made from the blood of poor people?'

Malik Bhago became silent as he realised the truth in Guru-Ji's words. Guru-Sahib then told him gently, 'Brother, it is better to earn a little with honesty than become very rich by taking advantage of other people.'

He continued, '*Akaal Purakh* has created all men as equals. It is our actions which make people high or low. A person who is truthful; who earns his living with honest work and is kind and caring towards other people, is actually the one who is dear to *Akaal Purakh*.' His words deeply affected all those at the feast. 'Because Lalo is so sincere and caring, is always ready to share whatever little he has and to serve others, he is close to Him. Therefore I embrace him as a brother.' Since then Lalo became known as Bhai Lalo.

Malik Bhago and many other rich men fell at Guru Nanak's feet and promised to live by his teachings. They became his Sikhs.

7

Guru Nanak at Haridwar

Continuing with his travels to spread his message to more and more people, Guru Nanak reached the holy city of Haridwar on the banks of the sacred Ganga. There was a religious festival going on there and the place was full of thousands of Hindu devotees. People were bathing on the platforms constructed on the river bank. Many were standing knee-deep in the river and casting handful of water towards the rising sun in the east.

Guru Nanak stood and watched this for a while; then he too waded into the river, faced west and began casting water in the opposite direction. People paused and stared at what he was doing and some began to make fun of the Guru. A large crowd soon gathered to watch and shout at him, 'Oye-you! You are throwing *ganga-jal* in the wrong direction.' Guru-Sahib ignored their taunts and continued casting water to the west.

Then a learned Brahmin stepped up and held his arm, 'Young man, why do you cast water to the west?'

'Learned sir, why do you cast it to the east?'

'O, don't you know? We are sending it to our forefathers in the next world.'

'Oh, I see' said the Guru, 'how far away is that place?'

'It is many crore *kos* (one *kos* is about two miles) away—
in the next world—but if we cast *ganga-jal* towards the
rising sun, it will reach them.'

'That's really great! Then let me finish my task of
watering my crops.' And he resumed casting the water
westwards with renewed energy.

'I am watering my crops in Punjab'

The bystanders started laughing loudly. 'He is such a simpleton!' said someone. The Brahmin again intervened, 'How far away are your fields?'

'Just a few hundred *kos*.'

'Then how can the water reach there? Can't you see it splashing back into the river?'

'Yes,' Guru-Ji replied, 'but the *ganga-jal* you throw also splashes into the river. Yet you say that it will reach many crore *kos* away and to a place which is not even on this earth but in the next world. Surely, if your water can reach your ancestors; then my water will also be able to irrigate my crops. These are on this earth and in this very country.'

He paused, observing the impact his words had made on the crowd. They now saw Guru-Ji in a new light—not such a fool after all! Some people began to sense the glow of goodness coming from him and their behaviour turned respectful. Then he asked, 'Tell me, why do you need to send water to your ancestors.'

Now everyone was puzzled. They looked at one another and thought, why indeed do we do this? After giving some thought to the Guru's question, the Brahmin said, 'Good sir, it is to honour their memory and give peace to their souls.'

'Those are indeed noble ideas; but blindly following rituals has no real value. If we *truly* wish to honour our forefathers, we should do good deeds—earn your livelihood with honest work; share a part of what you earn with those who are needy and remember the One who has created us all as brothers.'

As many, many people fell at his feet he said, 'What we give to help poor people and the kindness we show them in our life on earth really honours and gives peace to our ancestors in the next world.'

8

The Multi-crorepati

While on their travels, Guru-Sahib and Bhai Mardana arrived near Lahore, the capital city of Punjab. As usual, they selected a shady tree to sit under. Bhai Mardana started singing *shabads* accompanied by his *rabaab* and Guru Nanak-Ji also joined in. The sweet music floated softly over the area and lots of townsfolk flocked to listen. The *shabads* were captivating and the simple teachings expressed in Guru-Ji's songs touched everyone's heart.

Duni Chand, a multi-crorepati (millionaire), who lived in the posh part of the town, heard about Guru-Ji and thinking that the blessings of such a holy person would bring some happiness into his worry-filled life, he went over to meet him. As he bowed at his feet, he was shocked to find the Guru sitting on the ground under a tree.

'Guru-Ji, why are you sitting on the ground? Please come to my home and let me make you truly comfortable.'

'Sir, I am very comfortable right here in this cool, clean spot with a delightful breeze and birds singing around me.'

'Holy one, I have a big *haveli* where all the luxuries will be at your command.'

'I am not fond of big houses; all the comforts that I need, *Sat-Kartar* has made available right here.'

Duni Chand desperately wanted Guru-Ji to grace and bless his home. His face fell at Guru-Ji's refusal and he renewed his pleading with all his heart. Sensing Duni Chand's desperation, Guru Nanak agreed to accompany him home.

When they reached his stately house, Guru-Ji observed a number of flags on the roof. Duni Chand seated his guests on soft, luxurious divans and his servants brought delicious food which he served to them. Guru-Ji asked him, 'Why do you have so many flags flying from your roof?'

'Lord, they are a sign of how much wealth I have; each flag represents one crore rupees. So now I have seven crores.'

'Your vast wealth must give you a lot of satisfaction and happiness?'

Duni Chand was about to nod his head in agreement, when he decided to tell the Guru about all his worries that gave him sleepless nights. '*Malik*, (master) there is nothing that I can hide from you. I have this craze to keep on becoming more and more rich. There are many people richer than I and my heart burns to become the richest person. Also, all the time I keep worrying about losses and how I will prevent them.'

'So,' Guru-Sahib observed, 'those who are richer than

you want to become still richer, since they must stay ahead of you. There seems to be a race going on, isn't it?'

'Respected sir, I have no time to think of such things.'

'Would you have time to do a small favour for me?'

'It will be an honour to perform any service for you. What is your command?'

Guru-Sahib took out a needle from the small bundle he was carrying and handed it to Duni. 'Please keep it safely with you and return it to me when I ask for it in the next world.'

'Please return this to me in the next world'

A puzzled Duni Chand took the needle and later he told his wife about Guru-Ji's strange request. 'So, you have kept the needle?' she asked him.

'Yes, I have it with me.'

'Dear, how can a needle go with you after you are no more?'

'Not even one given by such a holy man?'

'Of course not! Nothing from this earth can accompany you when you are dead. You must return it to him first thing tomorrow.'

Next morning, before Guru Nanak and Bhai Mardana left his house, Duni Chand hurried up to him. '*Malik*, please take your needle back. I shall not be able to take it with me to the next world.'

'Ah,' replied the Guru, 'if you cannot take even a needle with you after you die, do you think all these crores will be of any use to you there?'

Duni went into deep thought, then asked Guru-Ji, '*Malik* what can I earn here that will benefit me in the next life?'

'Give away your extra wealth to feed the hungry, give shelter and clothing to the needy. Whatever you spend in the service of God's less fortunate creatures will be a credit to you after you die.' Then he told him to follow the golden rules and treat all human beings as brothers.

Duni Chand became a dutiful Sikh and kept using his wealth to serve the needy. For the first time in his life he became truly happy—even though he no longer remained a crorepati.

9

Where is God?

Guru-Ji had been on the move for twenty years and had journeyed East to Assam and Myanmar. To the North, he crossed the Great Himalayas and toured Tibet. He travelled as far as Sri Lanka in the South, covering all these vast distances on foot. He had many discussions with learned holy men of all faiths in India—Hindu, Muslim, and Buddhist. On the way he stopped to explain his beliefs and golden rules to the people in simple language and with practical examples which touched their minds and hearts. He also exposed blind rituals and told people to follow logic. His ideas were explained with everyday examples and so captivated people that large numbers became his Sikhs.

After such extensive travels he wanted to experience a Muslim pilgrimage (called *Haj*) to holy places in Arabia. So Mardana and he went to Surat on India's west coast and boarded ship to Arabia. There, in the holy city of Mecca, is located the Kaaba. In Muslim belief this was the first temple ever built, by the first man, Adam. Later it was rebuilt by the Prophet Mohammad himself. It is also the direction towards which Muslims face for their prayers or *namaaz* wherever they may be in the world. Hence, in India, Muslims say their prayers facing west.

Guru Nanak and Mardana put on the blue dress of *hajis*, took pilgrims' walking staffs and *lotas* (water jug). They followed all the customs of *hajis*. Landing at an Arabian port, they walked on to Mecca through the hot desert sands. When Guru Nanak reached there after such a long journey, quite naturally he was very tired. So, he lay down for a rest; but his feet were in the direction of the Kaaba. The locals believed that it is disrespectful to have one's feet towards Kaaba.

Many people passing him noticed this 'disrespect to God' and protested loudly. An excited crowd soon gathered around the Guru. One person named Jiwan, was extremely angry and he kicked Guru-Ji's legs. 'Who are you?' he shouted, 'how dare you lie with your feet towards God?'

'Brother, don't be so angry,' Guru-Ji said calmly, 'I am new to this place. Please move my feet where God is not present.'

His calm reply affected everyone deeply. Many of those who had gathered around, angry at this ignorant man, now had a glimmer of understanding about what he had really said. But, in the meanwhile Jiwan caught Guru-Ji's feet and roughly turned them away from Kaaba. As he did so, he had a vision of the holy Kaaba swinging

Rabb is everywhere

around along with Guru-Ji's feet. Again he moved the Guru's feet and again he imagined the Holy Kaaba moving to the direction of Guru Nanak's feet. Wonder-struck, Jiwan put the Guru's feet down and bowed his forehead on the ground before him.

'I saw God all around me!' he exclaimed to the crowd.

Guru-Ji sat up, his face alight with such a pure and adorable smile. 'Indeed! God and His house are in every direction, in every place and, if you look within your hearts you will find Him there. He is in your heart, just as He is in mine. The Creator is in everyone's heart, only we must make efforts to find Him. In fact, He is present within every living creature, be it plant or animal.'

Now all the *haajis* also bowed their heads as they realised how true his words were.

10

The Faqir of Hasan Abdal

After visiting Mecca, Guru-Ji toured through Arabia and many other countries before returning to the Punjab. Guru Nanak and Mardana came to Hasan Abdal, which is about 15 *kos* from Rawalpindi. There on top of a hill, lived a *faqir* named Wali Qandhari. Fresh water came out from a spring on the hillside and formed a small pool near which the *faqir* had made his simple hut. From this flowed a stream which met all the needs of the townsfolk.

Guru-Ji and Mardana sat down under a tree at the foot of this hill and began to sing *shabads*. Attracted by the enjoyable music, people came there in large numbers. The Guru explained his message of God and his golden rules and soon had a large group of dedicated disciples.

Previously many people would climb the hill and take along offerings for Wali Qandhari. However, since Guru Nanak's teachings touched a chord in most hearts, only very few persons now went up to him. Soon the *faqir* became jealous of the Guru and this made him very angry at the townsfolk. In a fit of rage, he decided to teach them a lesson for turning their backs on him and going to Guru Nanak. So, he made a small dam and stopped the stream from flowing down to the town.

This made life very difficult for everyone as now they had to walk long distances to collect a little water for themselves and for their goats and cattle. So, a group of them climbed up the hill and begged Wali Qandhari to release the spring water. 'Go to your Guru,' he said angrily, 'and tell him to give you water.'

Desperately they now approached Guru-Ji for help and explained the whole situation to him. 'Don't worry!' Guru-Ji assured them in his calm and confident manner. 'Have faith in the Almighty who will cool Wali Qandhari's anger and again fill his heart with kindness. He will surely release the water.'

Turning to his companion, Bhai Mardana he said, 'Bhai, please go up to Wali and request him in the name of God to free the water for the town.' Everyone watched the old man climb up the steep hill-top and eagerly waited for the flow to start again.

After a long, anxious wait they saw Bhai Mardana walking dejectedly down the foot path. Reaching Guru-Ji, he explained how he had conveyed the Guru's request to him. Wali had answered, 'Go back to him and tell him to arrange water for the town.'

Guru-Ji looked at Bhai Mardana, his companion for more than 20 years and now no longer a young man. 'Bhai-Ji, please go to him again and beg him in the name of God to have mercy on the people.' Again the people watched Mardana climb slowly to the hill-top. After some time he returned and sadly informed Guru Nanak how the *faqir* had angrily rejected the request. 'Tell your Guru to arrange the water himself!' he had said.

Guru-Ji looked at his old companion and asked him if he could go to Wali once again. Though quite tired by now, Mardana did not hesitate and began to climb up a third time. But even though the townsfolk were not that hopeful, they did not lose faith in Guru-Ji, sensing that there was a purpose in what he was doing. Bhai-Ji returned and once again conveyed how the *faqir* had even more rudely rejected the request.

'God is great!' he told the worried people, 'He can bring out a spring from wherever He wants. Have faith and join me in prayers to Him.' The people began to pray along with Guru-Ji and Bhai Mardana. After a while Guru Nanak stood up and went to a rock a little way up the slope. As he moved it aside with all his strength, water began to gush out of the new spring and soon flowed into the stream. The townspeople were overjoyed.

A short while later, the spring near Wali Qandhari's hut stopped flowing and dried up! Furious with anger, he pushed a large rock down the hill to crush the Guru. As it hurtled towards him, Guru-Ji remained seated and calmly put out his hand to stop it from rolling down further. It stopped just as it was about to smash into

Guru-Sahib. People had rushed to save him and were extremely relieved to see Guru-Ji safe. Then, 'Look!' one of the Sikhs shouted in amazement. The crowd saw where he pointed—there was a hand-print (or *panja*) carved into the rock!

Guru Nanak stops the hurtling boulder

Wali Qandhari witnessed these events and realised that the Guru was a truly noble soul. He was struck with remorse and running down the hill, he fell at Guru-Ji's feet and begged his forgiveness. 'Rise, *faqir bhai*,' said Guru Nanak, 'let your heart be filled with kindness and love for all creatures, like that of a true man of God.'

Then he explained that all men being created by *Sat-Kartar*, are brothers. 'Follow my three golden rules and serve poor and needy people.' Wali bowed before the Guru and his life changed forever after that.

Gurudwara Panja Sahib

A beautiful gurudwara has been built at Hasan Abdal and is known as Panja Sahib. The spring and *panja*-print still exist today. Many pilgrims, Muslims as well as Sikhs visit and worship there.

⤳ ⤺

11

Babur Conquers Punjab

Babur was a prince in present day Uzbekistan and was only 12-years-old when his father died. At once his uncle tried to kill him and become Sultan in his place. Babur was forced to flee from his capital, Samarkand, and find a place of safety in Kabul. Although barely a teenager, he returned to Samarkand by defeating his enemies but they forced him out again and again. Finally he settled in Kabul. However, he dreamt of conquering Hindustan, the land of fabled riches. How great would be the plunder from Golden Hindustan he wondered?

During the years when Babur was fighting his enemies, Guru Nanak was spreading his message of love among all human beings as brothers before God. After Guru-Ji returned from Mecca, he had met Wali Qandhari at Hasan Abdal. Now he came back to Eminabad and stayed once more at Bhai Lalo's home.

Meanwhile, Babur and his Mughal forces started their invasion of Hindustan through the plains of Punjab. While his soldiers were mainly interested in how much they could loot for themselves, Babur committed unspeakable cruelty to terrify the defenders into surrendering without much fighting. While Guru Nanak was still at Eminabad, Babur attacked and defeated the Muslim rulers of that area. He killed a large number of soldiers and took many as prisoners.

The townspeople were herded together and forced to carry all their own looted things to the Mughal camp! Although he had hardly any of his own possessions, Guru Nanak was made to carry a heavy bundle on his head while Bhai Mardana was given a horse loaded with more booty to take along.

Escorted by cruel soldiers, they walked along with a crowd of townspeople being taken to prison all carrying the booty robbed from them. Many were wailing loudly for their loved-ones who had been killed or sobbing to see the looters take away every valuable thing they had earned with a life-time of hard work. Everyone was terrified and bowed down with grief. Seeing their misery, Guru Nanak's heart was filled with compassion and he began to sing a *shabad* to God. His voice was so delightful that first Bhai Mardana, then some others joined in and the weight of their sorrows somehow seemed lighter.

At the prison camp all the prisoners were put to hard work. Guru Nanak and many others were given a heavy *chakki* (grinding mill) and some corn and told to grind it into flour (*atta*). The mood of the prisoners was downcast and some sobbed while they worked. Once again Guru Nanak began to sing a *shabad* in praise of *Akaal Purakh*.

It was so sweet and melodious that soon all the prisoners joined in and their hearts lifted.

The guards came to see what was going on and they too were charmed by the *shabads*. The prisoners began turning the heavy *chakkis* so effortlessly that it appeared as if the *chakkis* were grinding the corn all by themselves. The guards ran to tell Babur about the miracle they had witnessed!

'O holy *faqir*, what is it that you sing?'

Soon Babur came striding into the camp and heard the enchanting song and saw Guru Nanak sitting with his eyes closed, effortlessly turning the *chakki*. He was singing a *shabad* in a captivating voice. A hush fell around him as fearful prisoners stopped their singing.

Guru-Ji continued to sing but he opened his eyes to see Babur standing respectfully before him with folded hands. Although he did not understand the song, it filled his heart with peace.

Politely he asked the Guru, 'O holy *faqir*, what is it that you sing?'

Guru Nanak addressed him in *farsi*, which Babur understood. 'I was singing to God to see what cruel things you have done. Many innocent men and women have been killed and their homes looted. What harm had they done you or your soldiers?'

Babur remained silent, pondering the Guru's words. Guru-Ji went on, 'God has created all creatures and we all are His children. I am singing to Him to witness your heartless cruelty towards His innocent children.'

The Guru's words affected Babur deeply. He realised how wrong had been his actions, 'Holy man, how can I make up for what has been done?'

'Set all the innocent people free and return their belongings!'

'I accept your decision,' said Babur as he bowed his head before Guru Nanak. In his heart he felt sure that this man of God could help him realise his dream of conquering the throne of Delhi. Picking up courage, he again addressed him, 'I have set my heart on becoming the Shah of Hindustan. Tell me, O Holy One, will you pray for my success?'

Guru-Ji thought for a while, then he looked into Babur's eyes and saw that he was basically a God-fearing, if misguided ruler. 'Your wish will be fulfilled' he pronounced, 'but you must always be a just and kind ruler. Be merciful to those whom you defeat and above all, remember that God is our common father, we are all His creatures. Sing His praise at all times.'

In this charming way did Guru Nanak convey his powerful message of *Akaal Purakh* to the first Mughal Emperor.

12

The Guru's Langar

Guru Nanak had travelled to the four corners of the sub-continent and even beyond the Himalayas as also across the sea to Mecca. He had held discussions with wise men of Hindu, Islamic, and Buddhist religions. But most of all he had taken his message to the people in his own unique and folksy style. Entire neighbourhoods had gathered to listen to his *shabads,* which explained his message and his three golden rules in simple language. Now he was older and returned to his farm at Kartarpur. He discarded his saffron robes and once again dressed in every day clothes.

Guru Nanak back at Kartarpur

His Sikhs flocked in large numbers to Kartarpur, delighting in being with Guru-Ji. Now Guru Nanak put into practice his first and most important message: we are all children of One God and hence all brothers. Everyone who came to Kartarpur sat down together and shared their meal in the *langar*. They were one big family—Guru-Ji, his wife and children, members of his household and his Sikhs. This visibly broke the social barriers practised by upper caste Hindu society. Leave alone sitting and eating together, they never used to even touch low-caste people and called them 'untouchables'. The persons who cleaned their houses could not enter the kitchen. The Guru's *Langar* therefore, was the most important custom to prove to everyone that yes, all human beings (women and men) were created equal.

Guru Nanak worked on his farm and with his hard work he provided for his family and his Sikhs. Thus he practised two of his golden rules: *kirat karo* and *vand chhako*. Many devotees also contributed by sharing in the farm work; others—men and women alike—shared in running the *langar* and serving food to all who came there. Soon the hearts of these people lifted with great happiness in working for others. This was prayer in practice and they felt closer to God. Gradually the tradition of community service, (*sewa* in Punjabi), became one of the most important customs of Sikhism. Today, more than five hundred years after Guru Nanak started the *langar,* it remains a key institution in every Gurudwara and *sewa* has become a very strong social force, as we shall read later.

Guru-ka Langar these days

13

Guru-Sahib and Humayun

Bura, a small 10-year-old boy sat despairingly with his head in his hands and stared at the ruined crop in his family's fields. Along with his family members he had slogged hard in freezing winter mornings, in soaking wet rains and under the baking hot summer sun. This morning the Sultan's soldiers had mercilessly ridden their horses through the crops and set up camp in the still ripening fields. How would they now get food for themselves or for their cattle? With great effort he fought against the tears—big boys mustn't cry! Suddenly, he heard excited shouts, 'Baba Nanak is here!'

Men and women were rushing out to get blessings from the holy one. However, Bura first ran into his house and filled a bowl of milk; then he ran as fast as he could without spilling it, to where Guru-Ji was sitting. He fell at his feet and offered the bowl to Guru-Sahib. 'O protector of the poor! How lucky am I that I received your *darshan* (personal blessings) today. Please save me from the cycle of birth and death!'

Hindus and Sikhs believe that the soul never dies. When a body becomes old and expires, the soul merges for a while with the Creator, then is reborn in another form—just like we take off old clothes and wear new ones. Finally, when the soul has been purified with good deeds and following the golden rules, it merges forever with God (heaven).

'How lucky am I to receive your *darshan!*'

Guru-Ji was amazed and slightly amused to hear a young lad speak like an old grandfather. He thought to himself, 'Does this young boy really understand what is death and rebirth?'

Aloud he said, 'You talk like a wise old man, yet you are just a young lad.' Bura told him how the soldiers had destroyed the fields, 'No one could stop these cruel soldiers from destroying our months of labour. How will we feed ourselves? Who can stop death from slaying us all, young or old?'

'You are no mere boy!' Guru-Ji exclaimed, 'you have the wisdom of an old man (*buddha*). Guru-Ji blessed him and from that day he came to be called Buddha—Bhai Buddha when he became a bit older and later, Baba Buddha. Perhaps Guru-Sahib had an inkling that this young Sikh would live to be a very old and respected person. Bhai Buddha became one of the most devoted disciples and lived his life according to the purest Sikh ideals. He went on to serve the first six Gurus.

Back at Kartarpur Guru Nanak used to start his day three hours before sunrise with a bath in the river. Then, he would sing *shabads*, do meditation till it was time to talk to his Sikhs, who came eagerly to listen to his wise words.

After some years, he felt that his life was drawing to a close. So he decided to name his successor. Bhai Lehna was a very devout Sikh and quietly Guru Nanak put him through many tests and found him to be a capable and selfless leader. One day, in front of all the Sikhs, he seated him at the Guru's place and requested his old companion, Baba Buddha-Ji to put a tikka, a mark of Guru-ship, on his forehead. Then he bowed before Bhai Lehna, saying 'Your new Guru Angad, is a vital limb (*ang*) of my own body'.

Soon after this, Guru Nanak passed away. Guru Angad then left Kartarpur and went to his village, Khadur.

There he continued the traditions of Guru Nanak—the *langar*, *sewa* and worship of God. He too worked hard in his fields and by his strong examples many people flocked to Khadur and became Sikhs.

In the meanwhile, Emperor Babur had died leaving Humayun, his young son, as the second Emperor. However, Sher Shah Suri, one of his Generals, soon removed young Humayun from the throne. He was forced to leave Delhi, gather his scattered forces and struggle to win his throne back. He began to believe that if some truly holy man were to pray for him, he might succeed. One day, as he was passing close to Eminabad, one of his officers said to him, 'Sire, it was at Eminabad that your great father had begged Guru Nanak to pray for his success in his quest to become the *Shahenshah* (Emperor) of Hindustan. As you know, Sire, Allah-tala had granted the holy man's prayers.'

'Then I too will seek his prayers for my success.'

'Sire, his successor is called Guru Angad and he lives at Khadur.'

On hearing this, Humayun turned his horse and, followed by a small retinue of bodyguards, approached Guru Angad's home. When Humayun approached, the Guru was deep in meditation and the Sikhs were singing *shabads*, but fell silent, fearful of the band of approaching soldiers.

Humayun waited for Guru-Ji to get up and approach him, but he remained seated where he was. Humayun was visibly annoyed as he felt that a ruler should be shown more respect. Sensing this, one of his courtiers, who felt that a Muslim ruler ought not to be going to Hindu holy-men, spoke up. 'Sire, how can a mere Hindu *faqir* be so disrespectful to the Emperor. Give me the honour to punish him.'

His anger roused, Humayun drew his sword and spurred his horse towards Guru-Sahib, as if to cut off his head. Hearing the horse coming at him, Guru Angad opened his eyes and recognised Humayun, observed his sword, drawn to cut him down. He smiled gently, '*Shahenshah*, you draw your sword so readily to attack a defenceless *faqir*, but it has proved powerless against Sher Shah.'

The Guru's calm manner and soothing voice dissolved Humayun's anger. He now felt drawn towards this *faqir* who had such a holy presence. Even his bodyguards, particularly the one who had instigated Humayun, calmed down on seeing the Guru's tranquil and holy appearance.

Regretting his hasty action, Humayun dismounted and, handing his horse to one of his men, he now approached the Guru on foot. 'Holy one, please pardon my hasty and disrespectful actions.'

'My father had asked Guru Nanak to pray for his success and God had granted the Guru's prayers. I too

'May *Akaal Purakh* bless you.'

seek your prayers to regain my rightful throne. Will you pray for me?'

'I will pray that you succeed in your efforts; but do not forget God after you do succeed. Be a kind and just ruler for all your subjects; merciful towards your foes, since all humans are God's creations. Sing His praise at all times.'

Happily, Humayun bowed before Guru Angad and walked away from his presence. Only then did he mount and resume his campaign to regain his throne. This proved a success and Humayun became the second Mughal ruler of Hindustan.

14

Shelter for the Homeless

Amar Das was a prosperous shop-owner at his village Besarke, near present day Amritsar. His nephew was married to Guru Angad's daughter, Bibi Amro. She followed her father's routine of singing God's name before attending to her house work. One day Amar Das-Ji heard her singing some *shabads*. Finding them enchanting, he asked her, '*Biba*, what hymns are you singing? They are so enjoyable.'

'*Taya-Ji*, they are Guru Nanak's hymns.'

'How did you learn them?'

'From my father—he is now in Guru Nanak's place.' Fascinated, he asked for more details.

Amar Das was 60-years-old and had increasingly found that his life had become routine and without any purpose. So, he decided to hand over his business affairs to family members and go to Guru Angad for some time. When he reached Khadur-*sahib*, he loved the idea of *sewa*—working for others; of giving a helping hand to poor and needy persons. The concept of *langar* really appealed to him. This granted equal respect to all human beings, specially equality of women. Above all, devotion to *Sat Kartar* gave him a great deal of delight.

It was as if his life now had a direction, which he had missed all along.

For 12 years he found joy in devoting himself to serving others, doing *sewa* in the *langar* and sharing various duties of the community. One of these was to get up more than three hours before sunrise and fetch water for the Guru's bath. One pitch-black winter morning he was fetching water in driving rain and missed his way. His foot tripped in a hole made for a weaver's loom and he fell down. The noise disturbed the weaver.

His foot tripped in a hole for a weaver's loom

'Some poor fellow has stumbled into the loom-hole;' he remarked to his wife.

'Must be that poor, homeless old man, Amru. The Guru is also quite heartless to make an old man like him slog day and night just for some food and shelter. '

Guru Angad was upset when he heard about the weaver's wife speaking so disrespectfully of an elderly man and using an insulting short name for him. For 12-long years, ever since he had come to Khadur, Bhai Amar Das had been such an example to everyone that Guru-Ji had developed a deep respect for him. He was also well aware, that far from being a poor, homeless person he had left his comfortable home and life to serve the community. By now Guru Angad had also sensed that it was time to choose his successor and he could think of no one who could inspire the Sikhs with his personal conduct as Sri Amar Das had done.

One day soon after this, when the whole Sikh *sangat* had assembled, Guru-Ji seated Sri Amar Das in the Guru's place. 'Guru Amar Das will be the third Guru after me' he told the *sangat*, 'he is *nir-aasreyan da aasra*— the shelter for the homeless.'

Then he asked Baba Buddha-Ji to put a tikka on his forehead and himself bowed before him. In fact Baba Buddha-Ji would be fortunate to apply tikka to three more Gurus who succeeded Guru Amar Das.

⇝⊙⇝

15

The Greedy Merchant

Gangu Shah was a very rich and successful merchant in Lahore. He was extremely popular and his house was always full of relatives and rich friends. Like many rich people, he wanted to become even richer. This became his main aim and at times, he did not hesitate to make more profits even at the cost of other people, including his friends. Then came a time when he began to suffer heavy losses, which he blamed on 'bad luck'. Although he consulted many fortune-tellers, nothing helped. Maybe, those with whom he did business had got wise to his tricks. Soon he had lost all his wealth and had to sell off even his house. Now suddenly, all his 'friends' did not recognise him anymore and even his relatives turned their backs on him!

He decided to leave Lahore and start afresh somewhere else. On the way, someone told him about the Sikh Guru who was reputed to be *'nir-aasreyan da aasra'* or Shelter for the Homeless. Therefore, Gangu went to Goindwal to meet Guru Amar Das. Reaching there, he was so bowed down in his own hard luck that he did not notice the joyous atmosphere which filled the Guru's place. He stopped one of the Sikhs, 'Can you tell me where I can meet Guru Amar Das-Ji?'

The man looked at him with kindness in his eyes, 'Brother, he lives here; but all those who want to meet him have to first share the food in the *langar*. That is the Guru's rule.'

Gangu did not like the idea of eating with common people but if he wanted the Guru's blessings he would have to shake off his dislike and go to the *langar*. There again he found that as a high-caste *khatri* he would have to sit alongside Muslims and lower castes and share the same food. Again, he put aside his dislike and ate the food served to him, all the while cursing his luck in having to follow such unpleasant rules.

However, when he was taken before Guru-Sahib, he fell at his feet and narrated his tale of woe, how bad luck had suddenly come upon him and how all his friends had left him. Guru-Ji listened patiently, then asked, 'Were all your dealings completely honest?' Gangu started thinking how to reply to Guru-Sahib.

'When you were wealthy, did you help any poor and needy people?' As Gangu fell silent, Guru-Ji went on, 'You don't need to tell me, but only be truthful to yourself. Now go to Delhi and start your business again. Remember three golden rules: do your business honestly; help poor and needy people and take time out every day for prayers to Almighty. Finally, if you become rich, don't let your wealth make you forget poor and needy people.'

Gangu fell at the Guru's feet

Gangu Shah was thrilled to get the Guru's blessing, which he was certain would make him rich again. Accordingly, he started his business in Delhi with honest principles, strictly following the golden rules. Sure enough, his work prospered.

Meanwhile, a poor *brahmin* came to ask Guru-Ji for his help. His daughter's marriage had been fixed but he did not have money to meet the wedding expenses. Guru-Ji found that the man was honest and hard-working and he deserved to be helped. So he gave him a letter for Gangu Shah in which he asked him to give the poor *brahmin* what he needs.

'Go to Delhi and give this letter to Gangu Shah; he will help you.'

By the time the *brahmin* met Gangu, he had once again become wealthy and as before, he made profits at the expense of other people. He had completely forgotten the golden rules. When the *brahmin* presented Guru-Ji's letter to him he thought, 'I have earned this wealth with my own hard work and ability. Why should I give some to this man? If I give him money the Guru will keep sending even more people to me. Let the Guru help him himself, if he so wants.' Accordingly he sent the poor man away empty-handed.

Sadly, the *brahmin* went back to Goindwal and told the Guru how Gangu had refused to help him out. Guru-Ji gave him what he needed from his own pocket. Deeply grateful, the *brahmin* left and was able to conduct his daughter's wedding properly.

Back in Delhi, Gangu's greedy ways once again made him suffer heavy losses. Again a failure, he returned to Goindwal. But while he had realised his mistakes and wanted to beg Guru-Ji's forgiveness, he was unable to face him. So he began to do *sewa* in the *langar;* he learnt many *shabads* and constantly kept reciting God's name as he worked. Strangely, he began to find great happiness in working for others. The joyous atmosphere in Goindwal gave a lot of peace to his troubled mind. After watching him for many months Guru-Ji sent for

Gangu. As he came into his presence, he fell at the Guru's feet and begged his forgiveness. 'I had let my wealth make me blind to the needs of others, just as you had warned me.'

'You have learnt your lessons the hard way, but now you have become a true Sikh. Go and start your work again and live and work according to the golden rules. Help others too to do the same.'

Gangu Shah thereafter, started his working life once more. But this time he really got a lot of happiness in helping needy people around him and in following the golden rules.

The biggest lesson that his repeated downfalls from wealth had taught him was that life's greatest happiness and success lies in giving a hand up to those who find themselves down in life.

☜◯☞

16

The Emperor and the Magical Degh

Meanwhile *Shahenshah* Humayun died and was succeeded by his son Akbar as the third Mughal emperor. Akbar was the first of the Mughals to be born and brought up in Hindustan. Because the country he ruled had a vast majority of Hindus, Akbar wanted to learn about their beliefs. He also tried to have peace in the country for benefitting the public and decided to marry Jodha Bai, a Rajput princess from Jaipur. Because his policies were meant for all human beings in his kingdom, he became known in history as Akbar, the Great.

Akbar had heard how his grandfather, Babur had met Guru Nanak and requested him to pray for his success. Similarly, Humayun, his father, had received blessings from Guru Angad. At that time, Punjab was the gateway to Afghanistan, the Mughals' ancestral home. Hence, it was a key province and Akbar needed to visit it frequently. These visits took him close to Goindwal, where Guru Amar Das lived. One day Akbar felt the urge to seek the Guru's blessings. Going to the Guru's place, Akbar took only a small number of body guards and some men carrying a lot of valuable gifts for the Guru. They all dismounted from their horses and approached the Guru's house on foot. He was immediately recognised and one of the Sikhs met him outside the house and greeted him courteously.

'Shahenshah Akbar desires to meet Guru-Ji. Please escort him to the Guru's presence immediately.'

The Sikh bowed respectfully, 'Sire, it is Guru-Ji's rule that anyone who wishes to meet him shall first have a meal in the Guru's langar.'

The courtier who had spoken was astonished, 'But this is the Badshah of Hindustan. He sets down the law in his kingdom.'

'Respectfully, I will request his Majesty to first have a meal in the langar.'

The courtier turned to the Emperor, 'Jehanpanah, this is so disrespectful. Let us proceed on to Lahore.'

'No,' Akbar smiled at the Sikh 'I shall go to the langar, then meet Guru-Sahib.'

At the langar, his courtiers and body-guards were startled to find that they all had to sit on mats on the ground along with all the other devotees. But Akbar sat down without any fuss, appreciating that before God all human beings are equal. They were efficiently served with some daal, a vegetable and fresh, but dry roti. Akbar, who was used to the choicest dishes and delicious naan-rotis, soft with butter, hesitantly tried to eat some. To his surprise it turned out to be one of the most delicious of the meals.

Afterwards, while he was being led to Guru-Sahib's presence, Akbar reflected on the most unusual meal he had had, shared along with common people who would not have been allowed even near his palace gates. He marvelled at this extraordinary Guru with such great courage that he did not make an exception even for the Badshah whose one word could put him to death. Arriving before the Guru, he offered the valuable gifts that he had brought with him. But Guru-Ji declined to take them. 'O mighty *Badshah*, I really have no need for such riches; kindly give these to those who have need of them.' Akbar earnestly desired to do something for the Guru. He tried a different approach.

'O mighty *Badshah*, I really have no need for such riches'

'Holy one, how do you manage to provide food for so many people every day?'

'All the Sikhs put aside some part of what they earn to help needy persons. They also support the *langar*, both by contributing food items as also with *sewa* to keep the kitchen running.'

Akbar asked one of the *sewadars* who had served him, 'Which wonderful vessel do you use for cooking?'

'Sire, it is just an ordinary *degh*.'

'No, no!' exclaimed Akbar, turning to Guru-Ji, 'it is a really magical *degh*! It makes ordinary citizens sit as equals to the *Shahenshah*! It breaks down the walls which small men have raised inside their hearts—walls which split Muslims from Hindus; rich from poor and high-caste from low-castes. A true miracle of God! Therefore, I would like to help in running your *langar*—please accept the grant of a *jagir* whose income shall provide for all the needs of the *langar* and your Sikhs.'

'Your Majesty, I must thank you for your noble thoughts and good intentions; but the Almighty has given us everything that we need. The *langar* and the needs of our *sangat* must be supported by the earnings and *sewa* of the Sikhs. This is one of Guru Nanak's golden rules which Guru-Sahib had even asked your respected father and grandfather to follow.'

Seeing that the Guru would not accept anything for himself he said, 'As you do not accept anything from me,

I will like to give the *jagir* as a gift for your daughter—she is just like one of my own.' So saying, he gave orders for granting a *jagir* to Bibi Bhani, Guru-Sahib's daughter and fixed his seal on the grant.

Guru-Sahib presented him with a *saropa* and gave him his blessings, 'May your rule flourish and may the nobility and justice of your actions bring peace and happiness to all of Hindustan.' The Guru's words did indeed bless Hindustan during Akbar's rule.

Guru-Ji appointed Baba Buddha-Ji to manage the estates for Bibi Bhani. Its income was utilised only for the public good.

17

Baba Buddha-Ji

Baba Buddha-Ji had met Guru Nanak when he was a mere lad of ten. 'You are no mere boy!' Guru-Ji had exclaimed, 'you have the wisdom of an old man (*buddha*). Guru-Ji had blessed him and from that day he had been called Buddha—Bhai Buddha when he became a bit older and later, Baba Buddha. Perhaps Guru-Sahib had an inkling that this young Sikh would live to be a very old and respected person. Bhai Buddha had become one of the most devoted disciples and lived his life according to the purest Sikh ideals. Therefore, when Guru Nanak felt that it was time to appoint a successor, he had selected Baba Buddha-Ji to put the tikka on Guru Angad's forehead. Similarly, Guru Angad in his turn had called upon him to apply tikka to Guru Amar Das. Indeed, Baba Buddha was to have the honour of applying tikka to three more Gurus and came to occupy a unique place in Sikh history. As we already know, Guru Amar Das had asked Baba Buddha-Ji to manage the estate which Akbar had given to Bibi Bhani, his daughter.

Guru Amar Das had two daughters and he selected for their husbands the two Sikhs most devoted to Sikh ideals. So, when the time came for Guru-Sahib to appoint a successor, the Sikhs felt that either of his sons-in-law would be the most deserving to guide them as the next Guru. To decide which one, Guru Amar Das put subtle tests to both of them. In the end he asked Baba Buddha-Ji to apply the *tilak* of Guru-ship on Ram Das-Ji, Bibi Bhani's husband. Thus, he became the fourth Guru in 1574.

Guru Ram Das-Ji decided to have a large pool constructed on Bibi Bhani's estate. This would enable people to settle in the nearby area, which came to be called Guru Ka Chak. The lake itself was called the 'Pool of Nectar or Eternal Life'—*amrit-sar*. Baba Buddha-Ji not only supervised the construction but also joined hundreds of Sikhs in doing *sewa* for digging the tank. The berry tree or *beri*, under which Baba Buddha-Ji sat for supervising the work, still exists next to the *amrit-sar*. Guru Ram Das-Ji composed many hymns and under his guidance, hundreds of devotees came to follow the ideals of Guru Nanak. Their offerings and *sewa* for the Guru-house enabled the Sikhs to help even larger numbers of poor people.

Guru Ram Das-Ji found his youngest son, Arjan Dev to be most deserving of continuing the teachings of Nanak. He consulted with the Sikhs and then declared him as his successor before all the Sikhs present there. Baba Buddha-Ji was again called upon to apply tikka to Arjan Dev. But Prithia, his eldest son was angry with his father for 'denying him his right' and went away in a huff.

Amrit sarovar under construction

Soon thereafter, Guru Ram Das passed away and Guru Arjan Dev began his duties as the fifth Guru in Guru ka Chak. Meanwhile, Prithia wanted at any cost, to possess the power and riches given to the Guru by his Sikhs. So he started wearing the Guru-*tilak* and posed as the Guru. Since only local Sikhs could actually recognise the Guru, Prithia was able to deceive most visitors. He not only took the offerings which they brought, but also sent them to the Guru's *langar* for food. Guru Arjan Dev continued to provide the best possible food for the devotees. As the Guru's income reduced, he first cut down on his own meals. Many days he and his wife had to make do with just dry *channa* (roasted gram); at times they could eat only a little roti once a day. Naturally, after a while the quality of food in the *langar* was also affected. One day his wife asked him gently, 'Why don't you tell people about Prithia's tricks? After all, in front of everyone Guru Ram Das-Ji appointed you to lead the Sikhs.'

'Don't worry. In time truth will win.'

Sometime after that his uncle, Bhai Gurdas came from Agra to visit Guru Arjan Dev-Ji. He was extremely upset to see how poor the conditions were in which the Guru's family were living. So, he went to see Baba Buddha-Ji and explained the whole situation to him. Baba Buddha-Ji immediately sat down at the entry to Guru ka Chak and collected all the offerings of the Sikhs while informing them where the true Guru was staying. Once the contributions of the devotees resumed, everything was set right again and Prithia's fraud was exposed.

18

The Durbar Sahib

Guru Ram Das had constructed the pool which became known as *amrit-sar* at Guru-ka-Chak. Now Guru Arjan Dev Ji decided to build God's House or Durbar Sahib there. This would be surrounded by the *amrit-sar* from all sides. He requested a Muslim saint from Lahore, Hazrat Mian Mir, to lay the foundation stone of the structure.

Hazrat Mian Mir laying the foundation stone of Durbar Sahib

When this was completed it provided a central focus for the lakhs of people who had become Sikhs, drawn by the universal appeal of Guru Nanak's teachings. The building itself is square-shaped and with doors opening on all four sides. These signify that God's House is open to all four major religions in Hindustan: Hinduism, Islam, Buddhism, and Sikhism. For Hindus particularly, it meant that the House was open to four castes: Brahmin (priests, scholars), kshatriya (warriors and rulers), vaish (traders), and shudra (unskilled workers). This can also signify that this house of God is open to ideas from all four directions and indeed, all mankind.

Like the previous three Gurus, Guru Arjan Dev Ji followed the practice of Guru Nanak Ji in conveying their message through hymns; in the language of common folk of that time and even in regional dialects. Since many, many hymns had been composed by the five Gurus up to that time, he decided that all these hymns should be compiled in one book. So, he sent out word that anyone possessing the *shabads* of the first four Gurus should send these to him. Baba Mohan, son of Guru Amar Das, was known to have two volumes of *shabads* inherited from his father. However, he was at first reluctant to part with them but could not refuse when the Guru himself went to Goindwal and personally appealed to him.

These were brought in a ceremonial palanquin from Goindwal. Because the words of the Gurus were the very spirit of Gurus themselves, Guru Arjan Dev-Ji himself escorted them to Amritsar, walking barefoot behind the

Guru Arjan Dev and Bhai Gurdas Ji compiling the *Adi Granth*

palanquin. There, in a shady spot he and Bhai Gurdas Ji worked on the Granth. They included all the hymns of five Gurus as well as those of fifteen other saints, including some Muslims as well as some of lower castes. By including their hymns in the 'Word of the Gurus' he illuminated Guru Nanak's principal teaching that there is only One Creator and hence, wise teachings of holy men of any caste or religion are welcome. This belief remains central to Sikh religion. All the hymns selected also stressed that anyone can reach

Durbar Sahib

Golden Temple these days

God by living an honest life, full of love and respect for all fellow creatures.

By this time the Durbar Sahib had been completed and the Adi Granth, or First Book, was duly installed there. The Granth was respectfully placed in a cot and kept on a pedestal and Guru-Sahib insisted on sleeping on the floor beside the Granth. Thereby, he gave an example to all the Sikhs that the word of the Gurus deserves more respect than Guru Arjan Dev himself. Baba Buddha-Ji was appointed the first Granthi or Guardian of the Book.

19

Jahangir

Jahangir became the fourth Mughal Emperor after Akbar died. While Akbar had realised that Hindustan was a land of many faiths and he respected them all, Jahangir did not believe in this policy. By this time Guru Arjan Dev Ji had completed the Durbar Sahib, whose foundation stone had been laid by Hazrat Mian Mir, the renowned Muslim saint. The Adi Granth also contained the hymns of Muslim Saints as well as Hindu *bhagats* (holy men). Hence, large numbers of people from all religions and castes were attracted towards Sikhism. Some just listened to the *shabads* and participated in *sewa*; but many more became active Sikhs. This disturbed a lot of Muslim priests who did not like so many Muslims becoming Sikhs.

Jahangir

Similarly, many Brahmin priests also became jealous of the Guru's success.

The *mullahs* (muslim priests) went in a delegation to meet Jahangir. 'O, Your Majesty,' they said, 'please do something to stop this Arjan Dev as otherwise only few Muslims will remain in Hindustan.'

Instead of asking himself why so many people were being attracted to Guru Nanak's teachings, he started seriously thinking how to put a stop to Guru Arjan Dev Ji. He completely forgot how his great-grandfather, Babur and grandfather, Humayun had asked for the Sikh Gurus' blessings as well as the promises they had made to the Gurus. He even forgot how his father, Akbar-the-Great had become so impressed with Guru Amar Das that he had granted an estate to his daughter.

Around this time Jahangir's son, Prince Khusro, staged a rebellion against his father to try and become the Emperor himself. Jahangir collected all the forces still loyal to him and father and son fought pitched battles in which Jahangir was able to defeat the rebels. Khusro ran for his life from Lahore; was betrayed and put to death by torture. Jahangir, who had pursued him to Lahore, continued searching out those who might have helped Khusro and dealt with them mercilessly. Some *mullahs*, brahmin priests and others (like Prithia), who were jealous of the Guru, found this to be a good opportunity to end the Guru's influence. So they made up a story that Guru-Ji had given Khusro Rs 5,000 and also applied a *raj-tilak* on his forehead. Jahangir did not want to know whether the accusations were true, but found this to be a good excuse to put Guru-Sahib to death.

Guru-Ji was arrested and taken to Lahore where Diwan Chandu Shah, a high official in Lahore, asked to be personally allowed to torture the holy man. In the hot summer at the end of May, Guru-Sahib was subjected to unspeakable tortures for four days. One day, he was put in a large cauldron half-filled with water and boiled till the skin blistered; next day he was put on a large iron pan which was heated till his flesh burned with the red-hot iron. The next day this was repeated, while red-hot sand was simultaneously poured over his head. Chandu and the torturers wanted to hear him scream in agony, but Guru-Sahib fixed his mind on *Sat-Kartar* and kept saying, 'Your will, O God, is sweet to me.'

'Your will, O God, is sweet to me.'

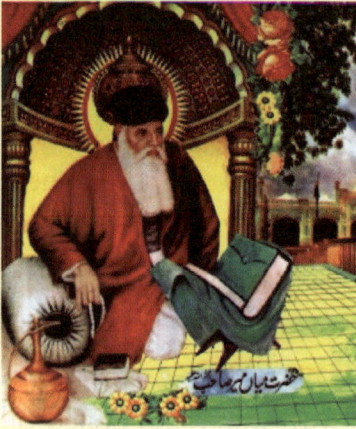

Hazrat Mian Mir

On hearing of the tortures, Guru-Ji's friend and devotee Hazrat Mian Mir, rushed to meet him. When he saw the ghastly scene, he cried out and said, 'O Master! I cannot bear to see these horrors!' He was not only a well-known *Pir* (saint) but was also greatly respected by Jahangir. He offered to immediately have the tortures stopped, but Guru-Sahib refused. 'Men who stand for truth often have to suffer. I continue to bear these tortures as they give strength to the cause of Truth. Go, my friend and pray for the triumph of Truth.'

On the fifth day, Guru-Ji asked to bathe in the Ravi river. Chandu at once agreed as he felt that the cold water would inflame the wounds even more. A huge crowd had gathered to catch sight of their Guru. He entered the river and took a dip. Then, he just disappeared and his body was never found. Many Sikhs who had come to catch a glimpse of their Guru said that they had seen a light flash in the river where he had taken the dip. A gurudwara now stands at the site where Guru-Ji passed away in the city of Lahore.

Guru Arjan Dev Ji's great courage continues to inspire people to stand up for Truth against falsehood. It also

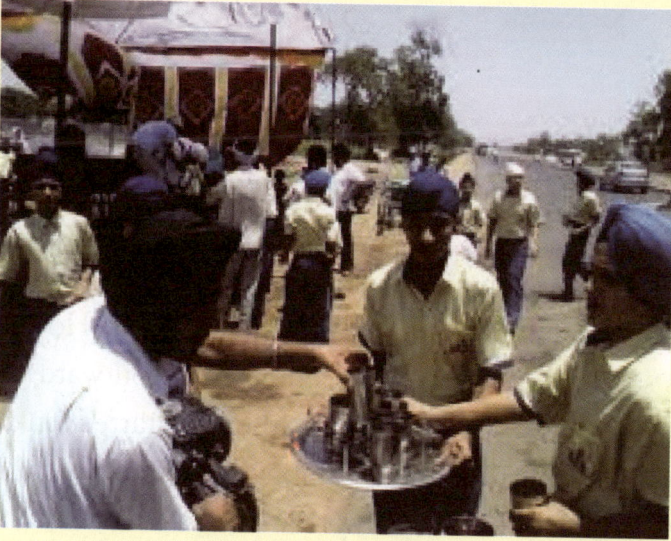

Sweet *lassi* to passers by

changed the character of the Sikhs from a peaceful people into soldier-saints—they realised that they could no longer meekly accept atrocities heaped on them, but would have to fight tyranny with all their might.

The Anniversary of Guru-Ji's sacrifice falls in June when, in Punjab, the summer sun blazes down with fierce heat. Stalls are set up on roadsides and all passers-by are offered cool, sweet *lassi* to quench their thirst in memory of his steadfastness, suffering and sacrifice.

🕉 🕉

20

Miri–Piri Da Malik

When the news of the Guru's martyrdom reached Amritsar, the Sikhs were overcome with grief. However, his son, Sri Hargobind-Ji maintained an outward calm despite the personal loss of his father. He started ten days of prayers from the Granth Sahib and *shabad-kirtan*, which was like balm to the raw sorrow of the devotees. After the prayers were over Baba Buddha-Ji came to install Sri Hargobind as the sixth Guru. When Hargobind-Ji had been seated on the Guru's seat, Baba Buddha-Ji applied the tikka to his forehead. Guru Hargobind-Ji looked up at him and said, 'Baba-Ji, it seems that we may no longer be allowed to live peacefully according to our beliefs and the teachings of our Gurus. Sikhs will have to stand up and defend their freedom of worship. From now on not only will the Guru have to be a spiritual head but also a leader in worldly affairs'. He then asked for two *kirpans*. He would wear one on his right to symbolise *piri* (Guru's spiritual role) and one on his left for *miri* (worldly affairs). His father had very wisely trained him as a soldier as well as in religious duties. Guru-Ji let it be known that those Sikhs who were able, should contribute horses and arms as their offerings.

Guru Hargobind, *Miri-Piri da Malik*

Thus, Guru Hargobind became known as *Miri–Piri Da Malik*. He became the first saint-soldier (*sant-sipahi*) and also raised an army of *sant-sipahis* who would act strictly for self-defence and righteousness. Soon the Sikh army alarmed the Governor of Lahore as well as Chandu and the *mullahs*. They decided to get Jahangir to act against him. However, keeping in mind how Guru Arjan Dev-Ji's martyrdom had inflamed the situation in Punjab, Jahangir decided to find out for himself about Guru Hargobind's intentions. So he invited him to a meeting in Delhi. He sent his messengers to Amritsar bearing messages of peace. Guru-Ji discussed the invitation with his advisors and his mother. They were afraid that this could be simply a trap. In the end Guru-Ji decided that he must take the risk and set up his camp at *Majnu ka Tila* a (few *kos* from present-day Red Fort).

Jahangir received Guru-Sahib with great honour and spent a number of days discussing religious matters with him. Guru-Ji made his points by quoting from the Adi Granth and *Shahenshah* Jahangir was convinced that he was a great and noble religious leader. A few days later he said to Guru-Ji, 'I am going for *shikar* (a hunt); would you like to come with me?' Guru-Ji agreed at once. In the jungle, a tiger had been disturbed by the Emperor's men and, springing out of the bushes, it pounced on Jahangir's elephant. The Emperor's escort shot arrows to repel the tiger's attack but did not succeed. Jahangir's life was in danger and he called out for help. Guru Hargobind Ji dismounted from his horse and tackled the tiger on foot. As the tiger turned to spring on Guru-Ji, he killed it with his sword. The Emperor was not only extremely grateful to Guru-Sahib but also found new respect for his courage and soldierly skills.

Back in camp, he thanked Guru-Ji profusely, 'You endangered yourself to save my life and have earned my eternal gratitude. I will no longer believe the false stories spread about you.'

'In the House of Nanak, there is only love for all human beings. We try to do good and be just to all.'

Chandu and others, who were jealous or fearful of the Guru's ever growing appeal and strength, had not given up. They cultivated the *Shahenshah*'s important advisors and whispered their fears and hate to them. In turn, these people kept sowing the seeds of suspicion into Jahangir's mind. For a king whose own son had revolted against him, Jahangir was essentially a suspicious man. These ministers played upon his weakness, 'Lord, the Guru has amassed a large army—Sire, he is so strong and fearless himself, his soldiers are ever ready to fight to death at his single nod—Your Majesty, he might soon be so strong that he could carve out a kingdom for himself.'

Ultimately, Jahangir forgot his gratitude to Guru-Sahib for saving his life. He forgot how he had admired his noble and saintly character and he ordered that Guru-Ji be arrested and imprisoned in the Fort at Gwalior. When he arrived at the prison, Guru-Ji found that fifty-two other kings had also been put in the same prison. However, while Jahangir allowed Guru-Ji to get his own food, clothes and other comforts, the condition of the Rajas was pitiable. They got hardly anything to eat and their clothes were in tatters. They would shiver without any blankets during winters. Guru-Sahib shared his food and clothes with them so that their health improved; at the same time he made do with little food for himself—sharing his little with the needy Rajas.

The news of Guru-Sahib's imprisonment on trumped up charges disturbed many pious Muslims and Hindus. Anger simmered against the Lahore Governor and

Chandu. In time, Hazrat Mian Mir of Lahore also heard about Guru-Sahib's imprisonment and he too was most distressed. He sought an audience with Jahangir. There he told him, 'Your Majesty, your regime is doing a great evil against a Man of God. When your people tortured and put to death the great Sikh saint, Arjan Dev Ji, he forbade me from bringing this atrocity to your notice. Now, you have imprisoned another Sikh saint. No good can come of such evil actions.'

Jahangir took the *Pir's* words to heart and ordered the Guru's immediate release. However, when Guru-Ji heard that he was free to go, he refused. 'Many innocent kings have been imprisoned here. I will only go if they too are set free!' The Guru's conditions for his release were conveyed through a messenger to the Emperor in Delhi and negotiations dragged on for several weeks. Many Sikhs pleaded with him to take the opportunity offered by the *Shahenshah* and return to personally lead the Sikhs. They were afraid that Jahangir might change his mind. But Guru-Ji remained firm in his resolve to get freedom for all the other prisoners as well.

Ultimately, a compromise was reached. The Emperor would allow only those prisoners to walk out with him, as could hold his hands or any corner of the Guru's clothing. He thought that now the Guru would be forced to choose only a few of the Rajas to save and leave most of them in prison. But Guru-Ji had a special cloak made which had fifty tapering points with tassels attached to each point. So, fifty kings caught hold of these tassels and two held each of his hands. In this manner all the prisoners walked free along with Guru-Sahib and Guru-Ji was able to get justice for all his co-prisoners. Gurudwara *Bandi Chhor* in Gwalior fort honours this event.

Bandi Chhor!

Mata Kaulan Ji

Soon after Guru-Sahib's return from Gwalior, Abdul Yaar Shah brought a girl to him for giving her shelter in his hostel for poor, homeless people. The girl, Bibi Kaulan, was the adopted daughter of *Qazi* Rustom Khan of Lahore. He had sent her to Hazrat Mian Mir for education where she had learnt some of the Gurus' *shabads*. Enchanted by these, she used to sing them at home. One day her father heard her, 'Child, what songs are you singing?'

'Father, these are Guru Nanak's hymns. I learnt them from *Pir* Sahib, Mian Mir Ji.'

'Do not recite these verses of the infidels (those who don't believe in God, as per muslim religion) in the future,'

'But father, *Pir* Sahib greatly admires the man you call an infidel. Surely, someone, whom *Pir* Sahib reveres, cannot be an infidel.'

He ordered: 'I do not want you to recite verses of these infidels even unintentionally.' Then he also gave her a sound thrashing. But as she persisted with singing the *shabads*, Rustom Khan consulted his colleagues and they passed a judgement, 'It is a great sin for Muslims to praise infidels and recite their words. Kaulan must be beheaded!'

Pir Mian Mir was appalled when he learnt about the order to behead Kaulan, and so he asked Abdul Yaar Shah to take her to Guru Hargobind for protection. Guru-Sahib made separate accommodation for her and also constructed a pond there, which became known as Kaulsar. Bibi Kaulan found the equality and freedom enjoyed by Sikh women to be a refreshing change from the restrictions she had earlier faced and so she became an ardent Sikh. In time she became widely respected and renowned as Mata Kaulan.

Mata Kaulan's pond; Gurudwara Kaulsar

21

Painde Khan

Guru Hargobind Ji's army consisted mostly of Sikh volunteers but also had many Muslim soldiers who got a regular pay. One day when Guru-Sahib was visiting Kartarpur, a group of Pathan (Pashtun Muslims) soldiers sought employment in his army. Among them was a very tall and strong lad of sixteen named Painde Khan. He soon proved his courage and skill as a warrior and also displayed excellent leadership qualities. Guru-Sahib not only selected him to become an officer, but also took special care that he got the best diet and training. He treated him like a son and gave him many valuable prizes for his excellent archery and swordsmanship skills.

Some years later, the forces of the *Subedar* or Governor of Lahore attacked Amritsar and a pitched battle was fought near Pipli Sahib close to the city. Painde Khan fought gallantly. His leadership played a big role in defeating the Mughal forces. Guru-Ji rewarded him richly. After a few years however, Painde Khan became very conceited. He began to boast that there was no need for the Guru to keep an Army, as he alone was enough to defeat any force. 'It is I alone who defeated the Mughals. If I had not been there, the Guru's Sikh soldiers would have fled the field.' Naturally, the Sikhs were extremely upset.

Painde Khan's boasts and hurtful comments reached Guru Hargobind Ji. He ordered that he would not be allowed to take part in any future battles but he still allowed Painde Khan to continue as an officer and to receive salary. He hoped that this would make him realise his mistake.

Soon after this, Guru-Ji was presented with a posh dress, some weapons and a beautiful hawk. He gave the hawk to his son and the other gifts to Painde Khan, telling him, 'I want to see you with these clothes and weapons whenever you come to me.'

Pande Khan's daughter was married to one Usman, who set his heart on having these gifts. Painde could not however give them away as he explained to Usman. 'Guru-Sahib has desired that I wear these every time I am called into his presence; hence I cannot give them to you.' But Usman conspired with his wife to take them away from his father-in-law. Not only that, he also took away the hawk from Guru-Ji's son.

On an early morning soon after, Guru-Ji summoned Painde Khan to appear before him. 'Where are the dress and weapons I gave you, which you were always to wear in my presence?'

'*Malik*, since I was summoned I came at once, without wasting any time to put on the dress.'

'Are you sure that these are still with you and not with anyone you know?'

'Yes, they are with me.' Painde Khan lied with a straight face.

'What about the hawk which I gave to my son? Do you know who has the bird?'

When Painde once again denied any knowledge, Guru-Sahib decided with a heavy heart to confront him with his lies. He requested one of the disciples to go and fetch the items. He soon returned with all the items from Usman's quarters. Even then, Painde Khan showed no regret and did not offer any apology. Guru-Ji decided to terminate his service and expelled him from his Durbar. Painde Khan became red with anger. 'I will complain against you to the *Shahenshah*; you will suffer like your father did!'

Usman and he persuaded 500 Muslim cavalrymen to desert the Guru's service, promising them a lot of plunder. They approached the *Subedars* of Jalandhar and Lahore and joined forces with them in an expedition against Guru Hargobind Sahib. A huge force of twenty thousand men marched against the Guru's Sikh forces, which were only six thousand strong. However, their spirits were sky-high. They knew that they had never harmed anyone and were just defending themselves against an evil attack. The desperate battle went on for three days and the Sikhs fought with death-defying courage. Guru Hargobind himself succeeded in killing the two *Subedars* and their army started running in disarray. At that moment Painde Khan charged at the

Guru himself, but Guru-Ji's sword cut him down.

In spite of the hard-fought victory, Guru-Sahib's heart was heavy at so many lives being lost on both sides by the rash actions of the *Subedars*. The pain of the wounded affected him greatly and he asked that those who had been injured should be treated. While riding around the battle field, he found Painde Khan lying with severe injuries. In an act of genuine compassion for all—Sikh or Muslim, friend or foe—Guru-Ji dismounted and went to Painde Khan, who was taking his last breaths. Screening his face from the harsh sun with his shield, he prayed 'O *Sat-Kartar*, in your boundless mercy please forgive this man.'

Guru Hargobind shielding the dying Painde Khan

22

Guru Har Rai— The Seventh Guru

Baba Buddha-Ji had by now become very old and he retired to his village where he passed his last days in meditation. Guru Hargobind Ji was at his bedside when he passed away. Then along with his sons, he lifted his body and performed the last rites. Today there are two Gurdwaras in the village, Jhanda Ramdas in the Amritsar area which recall these events. Later, when the time came for Guru Har Rai to be anointed the seventh Guru, it was Baba Buddha Ji's grandson, Baba Gurditta who was asked to apply tikka. Years later, he was also asked to do so for the eighth and ninth Gurus.

Guru Har Rai, like his grandfather, Guru Hargobind was an excellent horseman and soldier. But most of all he was extremely kind-hearted—a true saint-soldier. He loved helping others, especially the poor and needy. He also hated causing even the slightest pain or grief to anyone. Accordingly, he paid a lot of personal attention to the *langar*. Not only was the food hygienic and wholesome, but he ensured that the *langar* remained open all twenty four hours. People who reached even in the middle of the night could find a hot meal available to them. Out of his compassion for poor and needy people, he started a free dispensary for medicines. All sick or injured persons who came there were given treatment with care and kindness.

In the meanwhile Jahangir had also died and his son, Shah Jahan became the Emperor. He continued his father's policy of trying to counter the Sikhs, by stopping the construction of all new Gurdwaras and banned teaching of Sikh religion to Muslims. He demolished the *Baoli* for Mata Kaulan and had a mosque built over it. On four occasions his forces had attacked Guru Hargobind Sahib but each time they were beaten back.

Now, Shahjahan's eldest and favourite son, Dara Shikoh fell seriously ill. The best doctors in the empire were called to treat him, but the medicines they had prescribed could not be located anywhere. As Dara's condition became very worrisome, one of the ministers sought an audience with the Emperor.

'Your Majesty, I have learnt that Har Rai, the Sikh Guru, runs a dispensary which has an extensive stock of medicines.'

'You know that we put his great grandfather to death

Shah Jahan

and also had his grandfather imprisoned. We have also been attacking the Sikhs on many occasions. So, why should he help us?'

'Sire, I believe that he has kindness for all and his principal belief is to do good to others—even to enemies.'

Shajahan was astonished to hear this. 'Really? Can anyone be so completely good? This is absolutely unbelievable! Okay, send someone with a letter appealing to him to forget the past and ask for his help in getting the medicines.'

Guru Har Rai, not only located and sent the medicines, he also sent a rare pearl with instructions that this should be powdered and given to Dara Shikoh along with the other medicines. Soon Dara Shikoh recovered completely and Shahjahan, to his credit, vowed never to trouble the Sikhs again.

He nominated Dara Shikoh, his first-born son, to succeed him. However, as soon as Shah Jahan grew old, ill and feeble, Aurangzeb the third son, declared war on Dara and defeated him. Dara managed to save his life by escaping to the Punjab. Aurangzeb then declared that anyone helping Dara would incur his wrath. Dara the rightful successor to the throne of Hindustan wandered as a fugitive from village to village but no one dared to help him. Then he remembered how Guru Har Rai had helped to cure him and went to Goindwal and threw himself under Guru-Sahib's protection.

Guru-Sahib, himself a skilled warrior, maintained a small, defensive army of two thousand two hundred cavalrymen, as he had been advised by Guru Hargobind. But he was above all, a man of God and desired to have friendship and peace with all. However, when Dara Shikoh came to seek shelter from him, he realised that this could bring the Sikhs into conflict with Aurangzeb. But he felt that someone who asked for his help could not be turned away and accordingly decided to meet the fugitive Prince. Besides, Dara was also the rightful heir. The next day, they heard that Aurangzeb had despatched an armed force to arrest Dara. So Guru-Sahib sent his cavalry to the Beas river bank nearby. Since, this was on the road from Delhi, the move would deter Aurangzeb's troops from crossing over to apprehend Dara. This action proved successful and Aurangzeb's troops turned back without any clash. Hence, Dara was able to make good his escape.

23

The Saviour from Suffering

Shah Jahan was deeply in love with his wife, Mumtaz Mahal and when after nineteen years of marriage she died, he built the world famous Taj Mahal, where she was buried. Dara Shikoh was their eldest son and also the one whom Shah Jahan had groomed to reign after him. However, Aurangzeb, his third son, secretly nurtured the ambition to become *Shahenshah*. So, when Shah Jahan fell ill, he immediately launched a war against his brothers, all of whom he eventually hunted down and killed. His father, Shah Jahan, though old and ill, was still alive but he imprisoned him and assumed the throne as emperor. Of course, he granted his father's wish to gaze twice a day at his beloved wife's resting place, the Taj Mahal.

As soon as he became Emperor, Aurangzeb sought out all those who had helped Dara Shikoh, the rightful heir, or other brothers. People jealous of the popularity of Sikhs, told Aurangzeb how Guru Har Rai had sheltered Dara; how so many Muslims and Hindus were becoming Sikhs and also that the

Aurangzeb

Granth Sahib contained anti-Muslim remarks. Being very knowledgeable about Islam, Aurangzeb's curiosity was aroused and he asked Guru Har Rai to visit him and explain the allegations made against him. Since Jahangir had imprisoned Guru Hargobind, Guru-Sahib had made up his mind never to go to the Emperor. But it was impossible to defy the *Shahenshah's* orders. So, after much debate it was decided that Ram Rai, Guru-Ji's elder son, would go to Delhi and answer the Emperor's questions.

Ram Rai Ji duly went to meet Aurangzeb and was able to satisfy him about Dara Shikoh's meeting with Guru-Sahib. But, when some Mullahs asked about anti-Muslim remarks in the Granth Sahib, he could not give the actual meaning and said that the line was not quoted correctly. He gave a different version of that line. At any rate, Aurangzeb was quite satisfied and in fact, happy with Ram Rai. However, when Guru-Ji heard how Ram Rai had given a changed version of the Guru-Bani, he was very disappointed with his son as the Guru-Bani records the Gurus' actual words. He therefore, felt that Ram Rai was not fit enough to be appointed the next Guru after him. So he started grooming his younger son Harkrishan to succeed him.

When Harkrishan was just over 5-years-old, he became the eighth Guru, as Guru Har Rai passed away. Baba Gurditta was asked to apply tikka to the boy-Guru.

Ram Rai knew that he had greatly pleased Aurangzeb so he went to meet the Emperor and said, 'Your Majesty, I should rightfully be the Guru after my father's death, but instead my younger brother has been made Guru. How can a little boy be suitable for this; so, please pass an order to make me the Guru.' He probably forgot that Aurangzeb himself had killed his older brothers and snatched the throne! The Emperor decided to meet Guru Harkrishan before he made a decision. Hence, he asked Raja Jai Singh to have the Guru invited to Delhi to hear his side of the claim before giving a ruling. This pleased Ram Rai since Guru Harkrishan had promised his father, Guru Har Rai, never to go to the Emperor.

Raja Jai Singh had heard a great deal about the Sikh Gurus. He remembered how Guru Hargobind had made Jahangir free fifty two rajas and also how gallantly the Guru's Sikhs had fought the imperial forces. Hence, he was delighted with the chance to meet the Guru. But he also knew that, like some Rajput kings, Guru-Sahib had decided never to go before the Emperor.

So he sent a senior officer to Kiratpur to convey his own invitation to meet him. As instructed, this ambassador went before Guru-Ji and said, 'Maharaj, not only Raja Jai Singh, but all the Delhi Sikhs are eager to have your *darshan*. He has therefore, requested you to kindly come to Delhi and is looking forward to your visit.' Naturally, Guru-Ji was worried how to handle this invitation. His mother too was anxious that perhaps this was Aurangzeb's trick to harm him in some way. She also correctly suspected that this was Ram Rai's plot to get the Guru to Delhi.

Guru Harkrishan told the officer that as his father had forbidden him to meet the Emperor, he would have to decline Raja sahib's invitation. The Raja's ambassador stated that as far as he knew, it was only Raja Jai Singh's invitation; nevertheless, he would clarify if its purpose was for a meeting with Aurangzeb. A few days later, the ambassador informed Guru-Sahib that, 'Maharaj, Raja Sahib has placed his bungalow on Delhi's outskirts at your disposal. You will be his personal guest and he will ensure your safety. He has further clarified that if you do not wish to meet the *Shahenshah*, no one will force you to go.'

Guru-Sahib accordingly went to Delhi as Raja Jai Singh's personal guest. Delhi of those days was a walled city, present day Old Delhi. So, the Raja came bare-foot some two *kos* outside the city walls to receive him and escorted him personally to his nearby bungalow. Today it is the Bangla Sahib gurudwara in central New Delhi. Raja Jai Singh then told Guru-Ji that Aurangzeb desired to meet him. 'You know that my father forbade me from meeting the Emperor.' Guru-Ji told the Raja, 'Could you please explain this to Aurangzeb. It was his last command to me and I cannot disobey it.' Jai Singh nodded, as he had already guessed as much and promised to do his best to persuade the *Shahenshah*. After a few days he came to meet Guru Harkrishan again. He had succeeded in convincing Aurangzeb not to insist on meeting Guru-Ji. Instead, one of the princes accompanied the Raja to meet Guru-Sahib.

'Your elder brother, Ram Rai, has made an application to my father that he is the rightful heir to the *Gur-gaddi*.' The prince told Guru Harkrishan. 'The *Shahenshah* has sent me to get your views about Ram Rai's claim.'

'The Guru is not a king but a spiritual leader. The *Gur-gaddi* is bestowed by the Guru on the most suitable person and his decision is unquestionable.' He went on to quote examples from the previous six successions. The prince nodded in agreement, 'I see that your succession is perfectly in order and I shall convey this to the *Shahenshah*.'

Aurangzeb duly accepted that he should not interfere with the decisions of the Guru in their own spiritual matters. Still, he was curious to know if the boy-Guru had any special powers and he asked Jai Singh to find out.

Meanwhile, hundreds of devoted Sikhs flocked to seek the Guru's *darshan*. At that time Delhi was hit by an outbreak of cholera for which there were no effective medicines in those days. Thousands fell sick, while some people, mainly children, died. Many people now came to seek the Guru's blessings for helping them to recover. Guru Harkrishan gave them all some water, which he blessed with his own hands. As soon as many of the sick had recovered, they attributed it to Guru-Ji's healing touch. The news quickly spread and now thousands came to seek his blessings for recovery from sickness and for many misfortunes which affect rich and poor people alike.

Raja Jai Singh had been wondering how he would fulfil Aurangzeb's new instructions without causing offence to the Guru. His Rani suggested a plan, which would also enable her to get the Guru's *darshan*.

'Dear, why don't we invite Guru-Sahib to our home? I will disguise myself as one of the maids; she can dress as the Rani; then about a dozen ladies and some maids will give him a traditional welcome when he arrives. If he has any special powers he will surely pick me out from all the made-up Ranis.' Raja sahib agreed and so Guru-Ji was invited home.

Guru Harkrishan and 'Ranis'

About a dozen ladies, some of whom were Ranis, some women-in-waiting and some maids, came out with flower petals to receive Guru Harkrishan. He was quite taken aback as he was not expecting such a ceremonial welcome. 'I must greet the senior Rani first; so which one is she?' he thought in his mind. Then the next thought came to him, 'Why is there such an elaborate welcome? It must be to find out whether I am able to spot the real Rani.' As he walked up to the waiting ladies, he started observing them carefully. Then, from her regal manner he made her out! 'Ah, there she is, at the back with the maids. So I was right in my guess!' He walked straight up to her and greeted her. The Raja and his queen were delighted that the Guru did have extraordinary powers. This was duly conveyed to Aurangzeb who said he was fully satisfied that Ram Rai's claim had no merit.

Even though the people continued to come in hundreds for *darshan,* Guru-Ji who had been away now for quite some time, began making preparations to return. Unfortunately, he came down with small pox, a viral infection which has only recently been eradicated from earth. As he lay with very high fever, he knew that he was close to death and informed the Sikhs attending on him.

'Guru-Sahib who is the next Guru?' they asked. He thought deeply for some days, who should be the successor? Finally with almost his last breaths he whispered 'Baba Bakale', meaning that the next Guru (Baba) is in Bakala (near Amritsar).

In this way did Guru Harkrishan, despite being only a small child, win over everyone's heart and continued the tradition of helping out those suffering or in need. He became known as 'The Saviour from suffering'.

24

Guru Tegh Bahadur Ji

Guru Harkrishan had said that the next Guru is at Bakala, but had been too ill to specifically name anyone. Seeing this, all those desperate to be selected for Guruship, rushed there. So, when the Sikhs from Delhi and Kartarpur reached Bakala, they found more than a dozen persons claiming to be the Guru. However, only one could be the real Guru. These pretenders wanted to cash in on the opportunity offered, and started greedily collecting the offerings from gullible disciples.

Meanwhile, a Sikh named Makhan Shah lived in the Deccan and had a trading business of importing foreign goods by sea. One day he got news that one of the ships laden with his goods had been caught in a severe storm in the Arabian Sea. He became extremely worried because, if the ship should sink, he would lose everything. 'All is in the hands of *Sat-Kartar*' He consoled himself, 'in any case I can only hope that the ship survives the storm and wait for news.' He thought of the poor sailors and what would happen to their families if they perished. Then he started worrying again and so on, till he decided that if the ship should come through safely, he would go to Amritsar and make an offering of 500 gold pieces to

Guru-Ji to help the needy. As luck would have it, his ship survived intact. He was very happy and he at once set out for Punjab, to keep the promise he had made in his heart.

Reaching Bakala, he was puzzled to find so many claiming to be the real Guru. 'How would I know who is the real Guru?' he asked himself. Then he had an idea. He went to each one in turn and made a small offering of one or two gold coins. 'If he is the real Guru,' he reasoned, 'he will know about the promise I had made.' But to his utter surprise all those posing as the Guru, readily accepted his offerings without saying a word. By this time other Sikhs had found out what Makhan Shah was doing and they watched him keenly. But Makhan Shah kept the amount he had promised as a close secret in his own mind. When he had been to all the pretenders, he dejectedly sat down under a shady tree to plan out what he should do next to locate the real guru-ji.

One of the local Sikhs came up to him. 'Brother what is worrying you? Can I help you?' he asked. Makhan Shah explained that he had been to everyone claiming to be the real guru, but none of them are. After some discussion Makhan asked if there was someone related to the Guru families. 'Yes, there is one known as Tegha. He is Guru Harkrishan's grand-uncle, but he makes no claim to the Guru-ship.' the local Sikh replied, 'He meditates in total silence and may decide not to even meet you.'

Makhan went anyway to the house indicated. The door was opened by the man's mother and Makhan requested her to be allowed to meet with the holy man. She went inside and told her son about Makhan's request. Tegh Bahadur Ji agreed and so Makhan was ushered inside.

He bowed before the person meditating with closed eyes and placed two gold coins before him. Tegh Bahadur Ji heard the clink of metal, opened his eyes and peered at Makhan for some moments; then he smiled—a smile which sent a shiver of delight down Makhan's spine. He felt as if he had been wrapped in a cloak of great calm. When Guru Tegh Bahadur spoke it was in a very gentle way, as if he had met him earlier. 'Why, Makhan Shah, when your goods were sinking, you had promised 500 gold pieces?' Makhan Shah was overjoyed, because he realised that this was something that only the true Guru would know. He unwrapped coins from the bundle which he had been carrying from the Deccan, placed them before the Guru and bowed his head to the floor before him. Then he ran out of the house; scrambled onto the rooftop and shouted, 'Oye lakh, lakh wadhaayian! Guru ladho ray, Guru ladho ray!' The true Guru is found!'

Lakh, lakh wadhaayian! Guru ladho ray!

All the Sikhs came running to seek the Guru's *darshan*. They escorted him in a procession to the Guru's seat. Baba Gurditta came and applied tikka, thus installing Guru Tegh Bahadur as the ninth Guru.

ॐ ॐ

25

Guru Tegh Bahadur's Personal Example

Guru Tegh Bahadur was Guru Hargobind's son and grandson of Guru Arjan Dev Ji, who, as we have read earlier, had been tortured to death by Jahangir, Aurangzeb's grandfather. Guru Hargobind had established the tradition of *Miri–Piri* and formed an Army of volunteers to defend the Sikhs from being attacked and harassed. They had fought four defensive battles and defeated the Mughal forces. Now, Guru Tegh Bahadur realised that Amritsar was easy to attack because not only was close it to Lahore, the Mughal capital of Punjab, it was also in the plains. So, he decided to establish Anandpur in an area to the north, guarded by nearby hills. Since the Guru could not be present everywhere, he appointed *masands* for various areas and regions, to lead the devotees in practising Sikhism. People who could not give their offerings directly to Guru-Sahib gave these to the *masands*. These were collected and sent on to Guru-Sahib. It was these offerings that made possible all the charitable work and running the *langars*.

After securing the seat of the Sikhs at Anandpur, he left for a tour of eastern India, going to Agra, Allahabad, Patna, and Gaya. Leaving his family at Patna, he moved on to Bengal and Assam. Everywhere he went, thousands came to seek his *darshan*. Once people heard about Guru Nanak's principles and listened to the *shabads*, they embraced Sikhism in large numbers.

Meanwhile, ever since he had deposed and imprisoned his father and defeated and killed his older brothers, Aurangzeb had been fighting to put down one uprising after another in his vast empire. He succeeded in finishing off Shia rulers in the Deccan and even succeeded for a while in subduing the Marathas under Shivaji. Now, at last he had extended his empire to all of India, except the Deep South. Then he turned his attention to religious matters. He strictly observed all the outer forms of religion, its prayers and rituals. He even stitched Muslim prayer caps himself, which were sold to pay for the meagre meals he had. But at heart he was a very cruel person.

Could a truly religious person be so cruel and unholy; kill his own brothers and imprison his father? Unfortunately his view of religion was very narrow and he imposed a stiff tax called *jiziya*, against all non-Muslims—the vast majority in his empire—who were Hindus. He destroyed a lot of temples. Then he began to persecute the Sikhs and destroyed a few Gurdwaras, focussing on the Punjab.

This did disturb a lot of Muslims who believed that Islam was a religion of peace and tolerance. But, they were helpless against the might of the Emperor and the *mullahs*.

Guru Tegh Bahadur continued with his tour, though he was quite troubled. However, when Aurangzeb banned the *masands* from conducting prayer meetings of the Sikhs, he decided that he must return to Punjab to personally bolster the courage of the Sikhs there. Stopping at Patna for a brief goodbye to his family and young son, Gobind, he quickly reached Punjab. There he began a whirlwind tour, addressing lakhs and lakhs of Sikhs. Everywhere his message was clear. 'Aurangzeb has decided to make everybody in Hindustan a Muslim. He has appointed very cruel Governors and many Hindus, having been offered a choice of either being killed or become Muslim, have already chosen to convert. I am sure that sooner or later, his men will come to arrest me. I will be offered the same choice. You all know that I will refuse to give up my beliefs in the teachings of Guru Nanak and my predecessors.'

The Sikhs listened with heavy hearts, as they were convinced that Guru-Ji would not yield to Aurangzeb but follow the example of Guru Arjan Dev. Then Guru-Ji went on, 'Many of you may also face the same choice. If we truly believe in *Sat-Kartar* then have no fear and stand by your beliefs, as I am certain all true Sikhs will.'

His disciples would grow silent, each wondering if their inner conviction would be strong enough to make the right choice, when put to the test. 'My father had raised an army to defend ourselves and by grace of *Sat-Kartar* we have always succeeded in vanquishing those who came against us. So, face the dangers gathering like a storm with courage, daring and faith in *Sat-Kartar*.'

When Guru-Sahib was moving throughout Punjab and instilling confidence among the Sikhs, Aurangzeb was putting down yet another rebellion, this time among the Pathans of the Hindu-Kush mountain region. So, he had to wait till he was free from the campaign against the Pathans before he could move to confront Guru Tegh Bahadur. Meanwhile, he had placed the hard-line Iftikar Khan as *Subedar* of Kashmir with instructions to make Kashmir, then mostly a Hindu province, into completely Muslim. Iftikar Khan observed that the Kashmiri Pundits were very learned and influential, so he decided to first force them to convert. This would make lots of others follow their example.

He summoned the leading pundits and told them, 'You have a choice, become Muslims or face execution! Tell me what you decide by the day after tomorrow.' Greatly agitated over this life or death choice, they agonised over what decision to make. Some were in favour of converting, choosing to live rather than die, but the majority were for sacrificing their lives for what they firmly believed in.

Unable to get everyone to agree, they asked for more time and were allowed six months to give their final answer, or face execution. The months sped by but still they could not resolve their problem. Then one of the pundits, who had heard how the Sikh Guru had been preparing his disciples, suggested they approach Guru-Sahib. The Kashmiri delegation approached him at Anandpur and sadly narrated the terrible choice they had been given. Guru-Ji was plunged in thought about this knotty problem. Just then his son, Gobind Rai, came into the room, and seeing his father so serious, asked, 'Father, why are you so serious?'

Guru Tegh Bahadur and Kashmiri Pandits

Guru-Sahib smiled fondly at his ten-year-old son and, explained the problem to him.

'So, you are thinking how to solve this problem?'

'Yes, son; there seems only one way to stop these atrocities. Some well-known and holy man will have to make a sacrifice for them.'

'Who can be holier than you, father?' said Gobind, innocently.

Guru-Ji looked at him intently for a few moments. Would young Gobind be able to face up to the threats he would face after his sacrifice? Then he sighed, made up his mind and, turning to the Kashmiris, gave his decision, 'Tell the *subedar* that if he can convince me to embrace Islam, then you will follow.'

Aurangzeb was still busy putting down the Pathan rebellion, but being informed about Guru-Ji's advice to the pundits, he ordered that Guru-Sahib be immediately arrested. However, the Mughals waited till he went out with just a small escort. Then they pounced and arrested Guru-Ji and sent him to prison at Sirhind. When Aurangzeb returned from fighting the Pathans, he ordered that Guru Tegh Bahadur Ji be brought to Delhi. So, Guru-Ji and his companions were put in iron cages and taken to the Emperor. Aurangzeb asked the *Subedar* of Delhi and the *shahi qazi* to explain to Guru-Sahib all about Islam so that he would be persuaded to become a Muslim. But Guru-Ji had deep knowledge of the religion and he countered all their arguments with clear answers.

This was duly conveyed to Aurangzeb, including one view that the Holy Qu'ran itself stated that adopting

Islam should not be forced, but voluntary. But Aurangzeb ordered, 'Torture and kill his companions before the Guru's eyes. If they become Muslim, or suffer most horribly, he will certainly adopt Islam.'

So, Bhai Mati Das, Bhai Dayal Das, and Bhai Sati Das, the Guru's companions, were subjected to tortures too horrible to describe. All three kept reciting Gurbani and faced unspeakable suffering with utmost courage, refusing to change their faith. Then Aurangzeb told the Guru, 'True prophets have the powers to perform miracles. If you are a true prophet as you claim, then show us your powers.'

'True men of God never perform miracles to save themselves from death or to demonstrate their greatness. Do what you want, I will neither embrace Islam, nor perform any miracle.'

When he had thus defied the *Shahenshah*, Guru-Ji was taken from his cage and brought to Chandni Chowk, the world-famous city-centre. A huge crowd gathered to see the spectacle of a holy man being executed. People crammed the windows and balconies overlooking the Chowk. Guru-Sahib focussed his mind on *Akaal Purakh* and completely detached himself from the preparations being made for his execution and also from the crowds jeering at him. It was as if his soul was present away from himself and seeing these things being done to his body. Then the *shahi* executioners, brothers Bashal and

Shashal Baig, beheaded Guru Tegh Bahadur. Immediately after the beheading, Aurangzeb ordered that his head and body be put on public display and that he should also be denied the last rites.

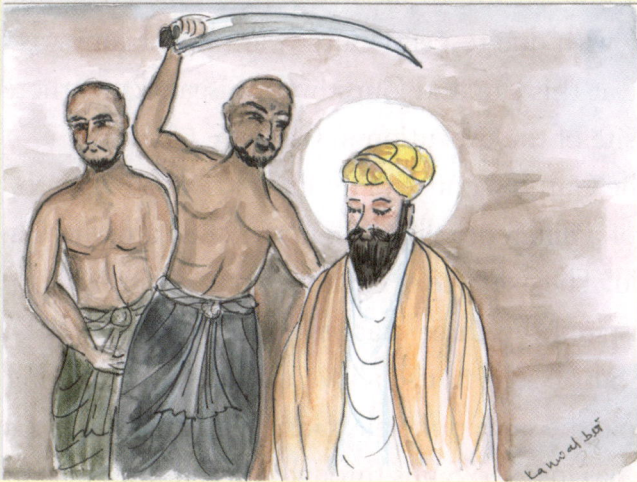

Guru Tegh Bhadur was beheaded

The Sikhs who had witnessed the dreadful events were infuriated but determined to cremate Guru-Ji's remains with sanctity. However, the site was closely guarded by armed guards. Then, miraculously a blinding storm engulfed the city as if God himself was expressing his fury. Taking advantage of zero visibility, Bhai Jaita was able to find the Guru's head and spirit it away to Anandpur Sahib. At Anandpur, Guru-Ji's son, Gobind, took charge of his father's head and cremated it with full rites. Even more daring was Bhai Lakhi Shah who carried away the

Guru's body; then placing it on a bullock cart, piled it with hay and took it through Ajmeri Gate out of Delhi city's walls. When Lakhi Shah managed to reach his hut he collected a pile of firewood inside it, placed the body on it and set fire to his whole hut, thus cremating the body with due respect. Gurudwara Rakabganj was later built at this site and Gurudwara Sisganj constructed at the site of the execution in Chandni Chowk.

The Guru's sacrifice of his life for freedom of faith, that too of a different religion, is unmatched anywhere in the world. The example of courage given by Guru Arjan Dev Ji inspired the three martyrs Mati Das Ji, Dayal Das Ji, and Sati Das Ji to rise above unendurable suffering and uphold the same principle. Guru Tegh Bahadur's example too, has inspired Sikhs through the centuries to stand up for human rights against terror and oppression. These sacrifices still remain an inspiration to Sikhs even today.

26

Guru Gobind and Syed Budhu Shah

As we have read earlier, Guru Tegh Bahadur Ji had decided to take Guru Nanak's message to eastern India. It was important that everyone realised that God has created all of us, so there should be love and brotherhood among all human beings. In fact among all creatures. He had left his wife in Patna and moved to Bengal and Assam. While he was travelling in this region his son, Gobind Rai was born in Patna.

There is a legend that when Gobind Rai was born, a Muslim *Pir*, Bhikam Shah of Karnal, got a strong urge to look east and bow. His followers were amazed, '*Pir* Sahib, when we all pray facing the holy Kaaba in the west, why are you bowing to the east?'

'I cannot explain, but I think a great *Pir* has been born there. I must go and find out.' So saying, he noted the time and date when he had got that insight and left for Patna. There he tried to find out which child had been born at that time. Finally, he went and waited on Mata Ji until she allowed him to have *darshan*. After seeing the truly enchanting child, the *Pir* placed gifts of sweets before the child contained in two identical, covered pots. Gobind Rai looked for a long moment at both pots then placed one hand on each of them. Then he looked up at *Pir* Bikham Shah and beamed him a sweet smile.

The infant Gobind Rai and *Pir* Bikham Shah

The *Pir* was overjoyed and exclaimed 'Wah! Wah! He will be a truly great man of God. He is destined for great deeds and will prove a saviour for both Muslims and Hindus, whenever either of them are in need of help.'

However, his followers who had accompanied him to Patna were puzzled. '*Pir* Sahib please tell us what you have observed that has delighted you so much.'

'I bought sweets in two identical pots—one from a Muslim shopkeeper and the other from a Hindu one. I covered both the pots and placed them before the holy child to see if he would favour either of the two communities. You saw that he placed his hands on both; then looked up and smiled at me—as if he knew. He will be a really great *Pir* and will favour all human beings equally. This has immensely gladdened my heart.'

Gobind Rai was only a small boy when news of Guru Tegh Bahadur's assassination reached Anandpur and he was anointed the tenth Guru. His father's sacrifice for freedom of belief inspired the oppressed Hindus as well as Sikhs. The Gurus, indeed all Sikhs, came to be regarded as protectors of *dharma* (moral law or religion). Many Hindu chieftains and Rajas admired and respected the Guru-house. Hence, it was that Raja Medni Prakash of Nahan, a small state in the Shivalik hills, invited Guru-Sahib to spend some time in his state. So, Guru Gobind Rai went to Paonta in the foot-hills of Nahan and on the Raja's suggestion, built a small fortress there. Later, he laid out gardens and made it a picturesque home. He spent many happy and peaceful years, composed many, many hymns, practised his warrior skills and went out for *shikar*.

At Sadhaura, some ten *kos* from Paonta, lived the Syed *Pir*, Budhu Shah. He was very keen to meet the Guru about whom he had heard such wonderful things. So, one day he landed up at Paonta and his first meeting so captivated him that he stayed on for many days. They held discussions on religious issues and the *Pir* was more and more taken by the Guru's views that all humankind are children of the same *Sat-Kartar* and hence brothers. Soon he became his devoted disciple.

Pir Budhu Shah meets Guru Gobind

On return from Paonta, he found a body of 500 Pathan soldiers waiting for him. They were professional soldiers in the *Shahenshah*'s army, but had been dismissed on account of a small misunderstanding. Now, without a job, they sought the *Pir*'s help. They vowed that they would be ever faithful to whosoever the *Pir* sent them and would never bring him any dishonour. The *Pir* knew that the Guru had employed many Muslims in his army, so on their solemn assurance, he gave them a letter for Guru Gobind Rai. Accordingly, Guru-Sahib took them into his army.

Soon after this, the chieftains of the Shivalik Hills States got very worried that the Emperor would turn against them for sheltering the Sikh Guru. They were also nervous about his growing influence, popularity and power. Their pundits also became concerned as large numbers of Hindus started turning to Sikhism. The pundits kept slyly hinting to their kings to drive the Sikhs out of the foothills. So, Raja Bhim Chand of Bilaspur started conspiring to attack the Sikhs along with some other hill chieftains.

Meanwhile, the Pathans whom *Pir* Budhu Shah had recommended to the Guru, got wind of the Hill chieftains' plan and four of the five Pathan officers decided to go over to the stronger side. They deserted the Guru's army along with the soldiers which each commanded. Only one officer with his men remained true to his word and stayed loyal to Guru-Sahib. Guru-Ji was very disappointed and informed the *Pir* of their treachery. *Pir* Budhu Shah was deeply pained, taking it as his personal responsibility. So, when the battle was fought, he along with his brother, four sons, and seven hundred disciples joined forces with the Guru.

The battle of Bhangani was furious and bloody. The Sikhs and the *Pir*'s men fought valiantly and routed the hill chieftains' forces; but the *Pir* lost two of his sons and several disciples. Guru-Sahib conferred great honour on and gave many valuable gifts to the *Pir*. He expressed his deep sorrow at the death of his two sons, but the *Pir* told him, 'Do not mourn for them, O True Lord, I am happy that they have earned their place in heaven, by being of some use to such a Holy One as yourself.'

27

Creation of the Khalsa

At the time when Guru Tegh Bahadur had been taken to Delhi, the Mughal Empire had reached its peak. By then Aurangzeb's brutal methods had also created many enemies which kept him busy putting down one rebellion after another. If he took his imperial forces to quell an uprising in the Deccan, the Pathans in the north-west would rise up and so on. As a young Prince, he had dethroned and imprisoned his old father and defeated and killed his older brothers to seize the throne of Delhi. So, how could he ever trust anyone with command of a large force? Therefore, he had to himself go and fight wherever rebellions took place. This had left the Sikhs in comparative peace, specially after the hill chieftains had tasted the power of Sikh Steel at Bhangani.

Guru Gobind Rai knew that these chieftains were smarting from their defeat and he soon learned that they were trying to incite the Mughal *Subedars* of Sirhind and Lahore to attack him. He realised that sooner or later the Mughals and hill chieftains would try to destroy the Sikhs. How could a small number of Sikh forces match the might of the Mughal Empire? He would have to make the 'sparrow fight the hawk.' He knew that his

Sikhs always fought with great gallantry, because their ideals of Humanism and Truth gave them strength. Still, he needed to create a body of Lions who would always stand firm against evil and tyranny. After a great deal of thought, he decided that he must create the Khalsa, or the Pure Ones.

Every year the Punjabi harvest festival of Baisakhi was celebrated with traditional zest at Anandpur. Guru-Ji gave a call that every Sikh who could possibly come, must make it a point to attend the Baisakhi celebrations of 1699 AD. Also, they were to wear their hair long and not cut their beards. He had carpets and durries spread over a large open space to seat everyone at this record-breaking gathering. He also had a beautiful, decorative tented covering or *shamiana* placed nearby. After the morning prayers, he disappeared into the *shamiana* and when everyone began wondering what was happening, he appeared before them. Then he drew his sword.

'O beloved Sikhs, this sword must taste blood! Is there any Sikh so faithful, that he can offer his life for his Guru?'

The congregation were dumbfounded and looked at each other in total disbelief. No one came forward so Guru-Ji had to repeat his call. Many people became pale with fear, then to everyone's relief, Daya Ram of Lahore arose and bowing before Guru-Sahib said, 'My life is at your disposal, O True Master.'

Guru-Sahib took him by the arm and led him into the *shamiana*. The gathering waited anxiously outside. Then, to everyone's horror, they heard the sound of a sword cutting though flesh and bone. There was a cry; then someone shouted, 'Look there's blood flowing out of the *shamiana*!' As people craned their necks to see, Guru-Sahib emerged and raised his sword, now stained red.

'Is there another true Sikh ready to give his head for me?'

No response! Everyone sat still, too stunned to speak. Many stared at the ground to avoid looking at him. Guru-Ji had to repeat his call and only at the third call did Dharam Das of Delhi, get up and say, 'O Holy Guru, if I am killed with your sword I shall attain salvation. I am ready to offer my head.'

As Guru-Ji took him into the *shamiana*, terror gripped the crowd and some even began to slink away. A few people went and appealed to Guru-Sahib's mother, 'Please stop Guru-Sahib from killing his Sikhs.'

She was appalled at hearing about the human sacrifices which were practised only by primitive barbarians. 'This has no place in Sikhism,' she thought. So, she sent a messenger to Guru-Sahib, but he refused to even meet him. As he repeated his call three more times, many people started leaving the place. Finally, five brave and devoted Sikhs had volunteered for his human sacrifice.

When he came out of the tent after the 'sacrifice' of the fifth volunteer, he was escorting the five volunteers.

'Now, *pyari sadh-sangat* I present before you my *panj pyare!* (five-beloved ones)' First, the crowd let out a collective gasp of relief at seeing that the 'sacrificed ones' were actually alive. This was followed by amazement because the five volunteers, now dressed elegantly with majestic turbans, were wearing the same type of regal clothes as Guru-Ji himself. There were more wonders to come as Guru-Sahib began introducing the 'Five Beloved-of-the-Guru' with their names

'Bhai Daya Ram from Lahore.'

'Bhai Dharam Das from Delhi.'

'Bhai Mokham Chand from Dwarka' (Gujrat).

'Bhai Sahib Chand from Bidar' (in present-day Karnataka).

'Bhai Himmat Rai from Jagannath' (in present-day Orissa).

Soon a buzz started softly as someone observed that the *Panj Pyaras* came from five different regions of the country: north, south, east and west, and they were also from different castes. Bhai Daya Ram was a khatri; Bhai Dharam Das, a Jat; Bhai Mokham a washer-man; Bhai Sahib Chand a barber and Bhai Himmat Rai was a water-carrier. Now everyone was excitedly whispering this to their neighbours. But wonders had still not ceased for the day.

Guru-Sahib seated them in a semi-circle around him, then took a small *degh* of water and began stirring it with a double-edged steel dagger called a *khanda*. (We can observe this at the centre of the Sikh emblem today). Consumed by curiosity, the congregation were craning their necks to see what was happening. He addressed them, 'I am stirring this water with a steel *khanda* and saying a prayer that all those who drink this *Khande da Amrit* will become Lions. We, who drink this *amrit* will become Khalsa (pure); will be known as Singhs (lions) and will belong to the Khalsa Commonwealth. We all will merge our castes into the Khalsa. In my Commonwealth of the Pure, everyone will be equal, from the lowest to the highest. Women will also be as equal as men.'

Mata Jito Ji, Guru-Ji's wife, heard what was happening so she took some *patashas* and said, 'Please sweeten the *amrit* you are making with these *patashas*; this will make the Khalsas sweet-natured.'

The Khalsa Emblem

Guru-Ji smiled fondly at her, 'You are so right! Along with courage and fearlessness; the Khalsa must be peace-loving and filled with love of fellow human beings.'

Now the *panj pyaras* stood in front of the Guru while he continued to stir the *amrit* and recite the prayers. Then he asked each one to fix his mind on *Sat-Kartar* and 'take-post' in the military fashion—kneeling on the left knee. He sprinkled *amrit* on each in turn, asking them to gaze into his eyes and loudly proclaim, '*Wahe-Guru-Ji ka Khalsa; Wahe Guru-Ji ki fateh.*' (May God's own Khalsa be ever victorious in fulfilling His will.) Now the Five-Beloved were asked to stand and take sips in turn from the bowl, passing it first one way then in reverse order, till it was empty.

Then, Guru-Sahib presented them to the congregation. 'I have created the Khalsa in my own image—in appearance and spirit. Behold my Five Beloved Ones! Each is a Lion, fearless, powerful, and courageous. Accordingly, their names will from now on be Daya Singh, Dharam Singh, Mokham Singh, Sahib Singh, and Himmat Singh!' With these measures, Guru-Ji instilled such courage and fearlessness in the Khalsa which enabled them to stand up and face the might of the Mughal Empire. The sparrow could now challenge the hawk!

Guru Nanak's fundamental principle was that there is no difference between human beings of any of the four Hindu castes or of any religion. So, he had started the practice of *langar* where everyone sat together and ate the same food. Guru Amar Das had even insisted that Emperor Akbar follow this custom before meeting the Guru. However, social customs and bias were so strong in Indian society that in many important things, like intermarriages or even visiting each others' homes, the same old divisions continued to be practised, even though Sikhism is a classless and casteless religion. Hence, Guru Gobind Singh's step in getting the Five-Beloved belonging to different castes and regions, to actually drink from the same vessel was a revolutionary step in making Guru Nanak's vision come true. The next step which he took was just as bold and far-reaching.

Now, Guru-Ji asked the *panj pyaras* to make a *degh* of *amrit* in exactly the same way as he had done for them. After it was completed, he stood with folded hands before them and asked them to give him *amrit*, in the same way as they had been given. They were taken aback at this request. How could they, mere disciples, dare to give *amrit* to their own Guru, whom they called *sacha padshah*—the True Lord? Guru-Sahib was expecting this reaction, so he explained, 'You are the Khalsa; the Khalsa is the Guru; so now I am your disciple; please give me *amrit*!' Then Guru Gobind Rai changed his name to Guru Gobind Singh—just as he done for the *Panj Pyare*.

Now, he gave out the five symbols, which would henceforth, distinguish the Khalsa. Their Punjabi names begin with the sound of 'k', called "kakkaa'. The *panj kakkaas* are:

- 'Kesh' or uncut hair, as worn by holy men in India and as the Gurus themselves had worn. (In fact paintings

'Please give me Amrit'

of Jesus and Moses also show them with long hair).
Thus these denote the essential purity or holiness of
the Khalsa character.

- 'Kanga' or comb, to keep the hair clean and tidy. This
  emphasised personal cleanliness.
- 'Kirpan' or sword. As Guru-Sahib had said, 'When evil
  exceeds all bounds, it is righteous to draw the sword!'
- 'Karha' or a steel bracelet; to remind the Khalsa to do
  only righteous deeds—also, that the hand may only be
  raised to fight evil or in self-defence.
- 'Kachha' or shorts; the Khalsa is ever prepared.

Next, he proclaimed, 'Whosoever wishes to shed his
caste and merge into the Khalsa; whosoever wants to
be baptised as a Lion, please come forward.' Thousands

stepped forward to have *amrit*. The *amrit* ceremonies carried on over a number of days, so great was the urge to join the Khalsa Commonwealth. Guru-Ji made no distinction among various religions or castes and indeed, between men and women. This was a first in Hindustan of that period. In Britain and USA, it took a long and bitter struggle in the last century for women to gain equal rights as men—and they achieved this some 230 years after Guru-Sahib had bestowed equality on Khalsa women.

Some legends of how Khalsa heroines repaid the trust placed in them by Guru-Sahib, will be narrated soon.

28

The Charm of the Khalsa

Sometime after creating the Khalsa, Guru Gobind Singh went to the famous Kurukshetra Mela. Large number of people flocked to listen to him. Guru-Sahib explained how Sikhism was based on love among all human beings as equals. He told the crowd about the many incidents of forcible conversion to Islam through

Guru Gobind Singh

terror and the oppression in their lives. Everyone had some personal experience of such incidents within their own close friends and family and Guru-Sahib's words struck home. Then his stirring call rang out and thrilled their souls: 'When evil exceeds all bounds, it is righteous to draw the sword!'

Inspired and encouraged by his courage and captivated by the classless Khalsa Commonwealth, thousands flocked to follow him.

The Kururkshetra Mela was well-known for the quality of horses which the breeders brought to it and Guru-Ji was able to buy some fine horses for the Khalsa cavalry. Some hill chieftains had also come there and professed peace and friendship with the Khalsa. But when they saw the huge numbers queuing up to join the Commonwealth, they got very worried. What was more disturbing to them was that along with some Muslims, many more Hindus continued to embrace Sikhism. Noting that Guru-Sahib was accompanied by only about a hundred disciples, they debated whether to attack him on his way back from Kurukshetra. However, they were worried that even so few men might prove too much for them. Then, it so happened that they came across two Mughal commanders, each with about five thousand troops who were marching from Delhi to Lahore.

The Chieftains lured them with promises of handsome riches and all the plunder they could take from the

Sikhs, if they joined their attack on them. So, Guru-Sahib was forced into a battle against fearsome odds—a hundred Khalsa versus many thousand Mughals and a few thousand hill troops. While one of the Mughal commanders, Alif Khan fell in with the Rajas' plot, the other took time to make up his mind. Perhaps the offer of money went against his soldier's honour. When he learned that Guru Gobind Singh was a Sikh *Pir*, Saiyad Beg did not commit his troops to battle, but stood aside watching the fighting. He observed the battle, fascinated by the gallantry and skill of the Khalsa and their Guru. Never in his long years as a soldier had he seen such death-defying courage. 'Each Khalsa is *sawai lakh* (over one lakh) soldiers!' he marvelled, then started thinking what could be the source of their extraordinary courage? Suddenly, four hundred Sikh reinforcements arrived from Anandpur and joined the battle, giving renewed vigour to the exhausted Sikh force. Jolted to the scene before him, Saiyad Beg thought, 'Why am I just sitting here, watching the greedy chieftains defeat this holy man? If I simply avoid fighting against the *Pir*, evil will triumph over good. I must actively fight on his side.'

He allied his forces with the Khalsa against the Hill Rajas and Alif Khan's troops. This turned the tide of battle and the Khalsa forces returned victoriously to Anandpur. From then on, Saiyad Beg became an ardent follower of Guru Gobind Singh. However, he still had not found out what was the source of the Khalsa's unmatched courage.

The hill chieftains efforts to kill Guru Gobind Singh or throw him out of Anandpur had failed again and again. Now, they appealed to Aurangzeb, telling him about how strong the Khalsa had become and also a complete lie that Guru-Sahib had declared his aim of converting all Muslims into Sikhs, and that he was planning to establish his rule over India. Aurangzeb was always ready to believe that every Chief was plotting to overthrow his rule. Hence, soon an imperial army under the able General Saiyad Khan marched against Anandpur. On hearing this, Guru-Sahib mobilised his forces. But because the Khalsa army was a citizens' volunteer force, only five hundred were present when the battle was joined. The rest had gone home to tend to their farms and businesses.

The Khalsa forces, which also had a sizeable number of Muslims, were commanded by General Saiyad Beg and fought valiantly. The imperial forces were commanded by General Saiyad Khan, who was *Pir* Budhu Shah's brother-in-law. His sister and her husband, the *Pir*, had become completely devoted to Guru Gobind Singh. Saiyad Khan had heard a lot from them about the Guru's saintly qualities. When he saw so many Muslims in the Guru's army, led by a Muslim general, he was stricken by doubt whether it was correct for him to fight against the Guru.

When Guru Gobind Singh came face to face with Saiyad Khan on the battle field, he immediately sensed the confusion raging in his heart. So, he flashed him a smile of friendship and advanced towards him. Saiyad Khan's heart told him to respond to the Guru's friendship, but his duty as the Mughal commanding general stopped him from doing so. He aimed and fired an arrow at the Guru and was aghast when he saw that he had missed, which he seldom did. Guru-Ji kept smiling at him and invited him to try again. Saiyad fired many arrows as the Guru advanced towards him, but they all missed—even the final arrow shot from quite close range. At last Saiyad Khan cleared his mental turmoil and, on the battlefield itself, became the Guru's disciple. He handed over command to Ramzan Khan, resigned from his post and retired into the Kangra Hills to meditate.

The furious battle raged on for many days. Once again Saiyad Beg leading the Khalsa forces marvelled at the matchless valour of the Khalsas. 'What inspires them to such heroic daring?' he wondered.

As the number of wounded and dying on both sides piled up, their screams of pain rose above the din of the battle. Wounded soldiers would be driven nearly mad from thirst—the heat and fatigue of combat combined with blood-loss from their wounds, made them crave for water. Many screamed from the agony of their wounds and the torture of overpowering thirst. Bhai Kanhaiya, a tender-hearted and devoted Sikh, used to tend to the wounded in battle. In those days water would be carried in huge goat-skin bags called *mushk*, weighing over two hundred pounds each. Throughout the day, Kanhaiya Ji would bring huge *mushk*-fulls of water for the wounded soldiers.

Bhai Kanhaiya Ji saw only suffering fellow beings

One day some soldiers complained to Guru-Ji about Bhai Kanhaiya and he summoned him. 'Is it true that you gave water to Mughal soldiers, helping some of them to recover and fight us again?'

'Yes, *Sache Padshah*,' Bhai Kanhaiya replied 'it is true I gave water to all the wounded. But I saw no Mughal or Sikh among them; I only saw suffering among fellow human beings.'

Guru Gobind Singh was delighted. 'Wah! Bhai Kanhaiya Ji, wah! You have truly understood the message of Guru Nanak!' Then he gave him a balm, 'From now on, you must also apply this balm to their wounds. It will help to heal their wounds while the water quenches their thirst.'

General Saiyad Beg too had been disturbed on seeing Bhai Kanhaiya helping enemy soldiers regain their strength. But when he heard Guru Sahib praising Bhai Kanhaiya's compassion for all human beings, he knew that he had just witnessed a supreme example of the Gurus' teachings. In a flash of insight he understood the reason for the Khalsas' miraculous courage. 'It is the magic of the *degh!* It sets their hearts free from hatred; this makes the Khalsa spirit supreme. Even the deadly enmity of a battle-field is conquered!'

When the battle resumed next day the Guru's arrow killed Ramzan Khan, but the Mughals still continued the fight. When Guru-Sahib saw that they were too numerous to be defeated, he asked the Anandpur town-folk to move into the fort and also withdrew his forces into it. The Mughals gleefully looted the town then decided to return to Lahore. But the Sikhs soon learnt that the Mughals had stopped on the way at Sirhind to celebrate their hard-won loot. Quickly a cavalry force was organised under command of *Sahibzada* Ajit Singh, the Guru's eldest son. This force raided the Mughals while they were celebrating their victory and returned jubilantly with most of the items looted from Anandpur.

When the Mughal force returned empty-handed to Lahore, Aurangzeb was furious and began an inquiry into the defeat. He himself talked to many soldiers to get at the truth. 'What kind of a person is this Gobind Singh?' he asked one trooper.

'*Jehanpanah*, he is a most inspiring commander, a father to his people and equal to one lakh soldiers.' The soldier answered truthfully, his admiration for the Guru clearly showing on his honest features. Maybe the compassion of Bhai Kanhaiyya had inspired such respect in his heart.

Aurangzeb immediately ordered that the man be dismissed from service. But he could not dismiss the soldier's words from his mind. His soul's conscience kept pricking him. 'Am I right in fighting such a man of God?'

However, the Emperor within him told his mind that if such a holy one could be persuaded to convert to Islam, then all of Hindustan could be made Muslim.

᠔᠔

29

Anandpur Besieged

'*Jehanpanah*, he is a most inspiring commander, a father to his people and equal to one lakh soldiers.' Aurangzeb had dismissed the soldier, but his words, underlined by the sincerity with which he had said them, kept ringing in his head. 'Since the time of my ancestor, Babur, the fate of the Mughal dynasty seems linked with that of the House of Nanak'. This thought flashed uninvited into his mind. 'Am I right in fighting such a man of God?' His soul knew what the correct choice should be. But he worried how should the *Shahenshah* of Hindustan act. After many days, he summoned the *Subedars* of Lahore and Sirhind.

'If we can make a holy man like Gobind Singh convert to Islam; then the whole of Hindustan could be made muslim! Therefore,' he ordered 'bring me Gobind Singh alive. But if we are not able to capture him, get me his dead body.'

The *Shahenshah* had made his decision.

These two governors, aided by the hill chieftains and others, mustered a force of over two lakhs. The Khalsa forces were barely ten thousand. Out-numbered twenty to one, Guru-Ji staged a fighting withdrawal into the

Anandpur fortress while once again evacuating the town and providing sanctuary to its residents. The Mughals besieged the fort, hoping to soon force the Sikhs to flee. But, the Khalsa was not taking the siege passively. Every night, a volunteer cavalry force would sally out and play havoc into the besiegers' encampments bringing back with them vital weapons and supplies. Soon, those opportunists who had joined the Mughals for easy plunder, lost heart and moved away in search of easier pickings.

However, after some weeks the hill chieftains succeeded in diverting the stream which brought water to the Fort. Now the Guru's forces and their families were in dire straits. The Mughals announced that if the Sikhs vacated the Fort, they would be given safe conduct into Punjab. Many started pleading with Guru-Sahib to evacuate the fort and accept the Mughals' offer of safe conduct. However, Guru-Sahib assured them that the Mughals would go back on their word and slaughter them, or sell them into slavery. Everyone accepted this painful decision, as they knew that Guru-Ji and his family also shared equally the hardships and the rationing of food and water.

Next the Mughals came up with another idea to weaken Anandpur's defenders. They announced that anyone declaring that 'from now on he is not a Sikh of Guru Gobind Singh' would be allowed to go peacefully.

Forty Sikhs of Khidrana, led by Mahan Singh Brar decided to make this pledge. Guru-Sahib was distressed to see some people so easily renounce their faith. He asked them to give a written and signed declaration. On the other hand, the Mughals were disappointed that only forty cowards had deserted the Guru. They were also finding it increasingly difficult to feed their troops and prevent desertions.

Finally the Mughals swore an oath on the Qur'an and the hill chieftains on the Holy Cow, that if the fort was evacuated, everyone would be guaranteed safe conduct. Although Guru-Sahib was still not convinced about their sincerity, he was persuaded by the many pleadings and the miserable plight of the children and women. He prepared to evacuate the fort. As a safeguard he organised some Khalsa cavalry to move ahead of the main body, other troops to protect the flanks and rear and asked the women to dress as men, for their own safety.

Now, the Mughals and hill chieftains showed their true colours. Disregarding their most holy oaths, they attacked the Sikhs. The main body, along with Guru-Ji's mother and two younger sons, was able to fight its way safely through the attack. However, their protecting escort, which was personally led by Guru-Ji, was surrounded in an open plain. Their only escape lay in crossing the Sarsa River which unfortunately, was flooded because of heavy rain in the hills. Many of the Guru's soldiers were swept away in its raging torrent. Nevertheless, a small number managed to escape to Chamkaur, where Chaudry Bidhi Chand made his *haveli* available to the Guru's remnant force. This residence had been built on a small hillock and thus had the best defence in the area. They stocked up with supplies, arrows and weapons in the little time available before they were surrounded by jubilant Mughal troops. All of them were greedily looking forward to fat rewards and promotions from the Emperor, if only Guru Gobind Singh could be captured or killed.

Guru Gobind Singh, *Sahibzadas* Ajit and Jujhar at Chamkaur

Still, the gallant Khalsas kept the enemy at bay by continuous volleys of well-aimed arrows. Finally, their arrows exhausted, it seemed that the Mughals would simply run over the *haveli*; their Guru-Ji would be captured or killed and his body disrespected. It was then decided that the Khalsas would go out in batches of five and engage the Mughal force. The first batch fearlessly engaged the enemy with great ferocity and inflicted very heavy losses, before their small numbers could be cut down. The enemy were taken aback by the heavy casualties and they fell back to organise another assault on the *haveli*. But, even as their assault was beginning to form, the next batch of five Khalsas came at them, disrupting the assault and inflicting even more casualties on the Mughals before themselves embracing martyrdom.

Then Guru-Ji's eldest son, *Sahibzada* Ajit Singh, demanded that he should lead the next batch of five volunteers. Guru-Ji was immensely proud and happy to have such a brave son and spirited Khalsa. However, it was with a heavy heart that he personally strapped his weapons on him and saw him go out to fight to the end. Guru-Ji watched the battle as the brave lad fought valiantly against experienced Mughal fighters. When his horse was cut down, he assaulted the enemy with his sword. At last he was felled, but there was a huge pile of victims all around him. Guru-Ji thanked Almighty that he had given his son the opportunity to die for the cause of His Khalsa.

Guru-Ji had no time to mourn for his first-born as *Sahibzada* Jujhar Singh, his second son, inspired by the gallantry of his elder brother, immediately demanded that he should go out next to fulfil his duty as a warrior of the Khalsa. The remaining Sikhs were filled with misgivings that one so young would face experienced and well-equipped Mughal soldiers. But Guru-Ji at once agreed that he should go. When some protested that he should not lose two of his sons, he said, 'All my Khalsas are equally my sons.' The young *Sahibzada* Jujhar Singh, not yet a teenager, fought like a tiger and Guru-Ji had a lump in his throat as he watched with pride and fondness his young Singh tear into the enemy and ultimately fall against the tidal wave of enemy soldiers who came at his small band of Khalsa warriors.

Now, only a dozen Sikhs were left as the others had all been killed in going out after the Mughals. Those who had been martyred included three of the five *panj pyare* and the two *Sahibzadas*. The small handful of remaining Sikhs, impatiently awaiting their turn, were dismayed when Guru-Sahib announced his decision to go out with the next batch of five warriors. They felt that if Guru-Ji would be killed or captured, the Khalsa cause and its fight for freedom of worship would be seriously affected. They became subdued and quietly debated how to make Guru-Ji change his mind.

So, five Sikhs, including the two remaining *panj pyare*, constituted a Council. They said to Guru-Sahib, 'When creating the Khalsa, you had said, 'I am of the Khalsa, and the Khalsa is mine'. You then bowed before the *panj pyare* to be initiated as a Khalsa. Today we recall your words and as the Khalsa Council at this time, we beg you to make good your escape from Chamkaur to continue leading the struggle for justice and the Khalsa cause.'

Guru-Ji had no choice but to accept this decision. It was, after all, his own rule.

ᗞᗧ

30

A Horrible Crime

Abdul, the Mughal look-out, shivered in his campaign blanket in the chill of the cold December dawn. Then he heard a faint sound and cocked his head to one side to listen better. Ah! There it was again—he had felt sure that the next batch would come again soon, seeking to use the mist and darkness to slink away. 'Crafty soldiers, these Sikhs,' he thought, 'but Wallah! They fight like Shaitan himself.' He squinted in the grey light of dawn through the thick coverlet of winter fog and they were quite close when he spied them. His eyes opened wide with amazement and he shouted exultantly at his companions, 'Oye hurry, it is Gobind Singh himself! We mustn't let him get away!' Vaulting into the saddle, he licked his lips in anticipation of the fat reward which the *Shahenshah* would surely give, if only they captured or even killed him. His companions, dozing huddled in their blankets began to rouse themselves, get mounted on their horses and hurry to catch-up with those galloping to meet the Sikhs. Everyone wanted to be the one to capture or kill the Sikh leader. But the Khalsa *jatha* was in no mood to fall-in with their wishes. Even as Abdul spurred his horse forward, he was met by cold Sikh steel as the Khalsa tore into him. Abdul was cut down, still dreaming of rich rewards and the Mughals who came at them in turn also met the same fate. Then the Khalsa troop formed a screen protecting their leader with the *kalgi* (a jewelled plume) in his turban. The Mughal soldiers watched in dismay as the leader on a blue-roan steed turned away and rode off at great speed, with only three companions.

The Mughal commander who had now come up, observed the leader galloping away. He at once ordered his reserve troop to cut-off the bid to break-out of the encirclement. 'On no account must he get-away,' he warned his men, 'or you will pay with your lives!' He knew that his own head would certainly be at risk if the Sikh leader escaped. After about an hour of fierce fighting, he was relieved as all the Sikhs had been cut down. His only regret was that the Sikh Guru had not been caught alive. He entered the *haveli* on the hill in triumph to find it deserted, and the body of their leader laid out for his inspection. He saw the turban with a *kalgi* and the handsome features of the leader and felt a great sense of relief and exultation.

'Inform the *Subedar* that Gobind Singh has been killed!'

The next day, Khwaja Mardud of Chamkaur saw the body of the 'Guru' and exclaimed, 'This is not Guru Gobind Singh!' The *Subedar* at Sirhind was at once informed and he immediately ordered that check-points be established and parties despatched to hunt down the escaped leader.

Earlier, Bhai Sohail Singh, whose build resembled *Guru-Ji's* had offered to change into his clothes and sally out of the fort as a decoy, while Guru-Ji and three companions made good their escape in the dead of night. The body that the Mughal commander saw was that of Bhai Sohail Singh.

After escaping from Chamkaur, Guru-Ji wandered about for a few days, avoiding villages and hamlets lest someone give him away. Then he met two Pathans— Ghani Khan and Nabi Khan, who had lived near Anandpur and were *Pir* Budhu Shah's followers. They knew about Guru-Ji and offered to carry him to safety. *Mai* Gurdevi had spun a cloak for Guru-Ji, which was dyed in blue so that Guru-Ji would appear like a Muslim *fakir.* Then Ghani and Nabi Khan carried him in a palanquin along with Man Singh and Dharam Singh while Daya Singh waved the *chaur.* They soon encountered a check-point of the Imperial Army searching for Guru Gobind Singh. When asked who was being carried with such respect, the Pathans told the commander that he was their *Uch ka Pir*—which was exactly the truth! Soon Guru-Ji reached the Lakhi forest, where he gratefully bid goodbye to the two loyal Pathans.

It was here that Guru-Ji got news of the terrible crime committed by Wazir Khan, the *Subedar* of Sirhind. The two young *Sahibzadas* and their grandmother had been discovered from Saheri, near Morinda, where they had taken refuge with their cook, Gangu, who had worked for the family for decades. The captured *Sahibzadas* Fateh Singh and Zorawar Singh—aged six and eight years—were brought before the *Subedar* and asked to convert to Islam.

Wazir Khan spoke soothingly to the two children. 'You are both obviously very brave and intelligent little boys. I want to give you a prize—we will give you a grand house to stay with your *Dadi* and *Ammi*. I will also go myself to the Emperor and ask him to spare your father's life.'

But the two children were firm. 'We are the grandsons of Guru Tegh Bahadur, who was killed by Aurangzeb because he didn't change his religion.' *Sahibzada* Zorawar Singh spoke in a clear, firm voice, 'We will not change our religion.'

Then Wazir Khan addressed little Fateh. 'Your brother will die if he remains obstinate. You must accept my offer and I will spare the life of your *Dadi* and all your family members. Don't you want to save their lives?'

Six-year-old Fateh also spoke in a clear and firm voice, 'I am the son of Guru Gobind Singh and I will not change my belief. You may kill me if you want!'

Frustrated, Wazir Khan pronounced their death sentence, 'Unless you become Muslim, you will be executed!'

Sher Khan, the Nawab of Maler Kotla, was the only one to oppose this monstrous crime. '*Jenab Subedar Sahib*,' he said, 'we are *Musalmans* and Islam does not teach us to make war on women and children.' So saying, he left the *Subedar*'s courtroom.

Following the sentence, the two *Sahibzadas* were bricked up alive. As each layer of bricks was laid, the *maulvi* offered to release them if they converted. For three days the two boys had steadfastly refused, till ultimately the last brick had been put in place. Then they were beheaded by Bashal and Shashal Baig, the same ones who had executed Guru Tegh Bahadur Ji.

Defiant young Sahibzadas being bricked alive

Their old Grandmother could not bear this tragedy, losing all four of her beloved grandsons and it broke her heart. She too breathed her last shortly afterwards.

The news of the vile execution of the young *Sahibzadas* sent shock-waves throughout the land. Guru-Sahib, still in the Lakhi forest began to once again to receive offerings of weapons and horses. Meanwhile, he decided to tell the *Shahenshah* of the barbaric acts against women and children committed in his name by his *Subedars*. He wrote him a defiant letter demanding justice. This has become renowned in Sikh legend as the *zafarnama* or 'letter declaring victory'. While recounting all the crimes committed, particularly against defenceless women and children, it also describes how the Mughals broke their holy oath at Anandpur Sahib. He vowed to exact retribution for these crimes. He sent Bhai Daya Singh and Dharam Singh to deliver the *zafarnama* to the Emperor, instructing them to boldly tell the truth to him as detailed in the letter.

31

Forgiveness for the Traitors

When she heard the news of Anandpur's fall and young *Sahibzadas'* martyrdom, Bhag Kaur (popularly called *Mai* Bhago), a devoted Khalsa lady living near Amritsar, was shocked that the Khalsas at Anandpur had come through a test of fire while most people in neighbouring villages had just stayed on in their homes. She was even more furious to learn that forty Sikhs of Khidrana had deserted Guru-Ji at Anandpur in the hour of the Khalsa's greatest need. She and her husband began rousing village after village around Amritsar. They recounted the sacrifices made by the Guru's family and the shameful desertion by those forty turncoats. Women of all neighbouring villages decided to refuse the forty deserters any food or shelter, or allow any of them into their homes.

Mai Bhago said, 'Guru-Ji has sacrificed his family and comforts for our freedom. It's now time for all of us to stand up and protect our rights and faith. Why not die a gallant death instead of meekly awaiting our turn to be crushed.' She challenged the men, 'If you don't join me, I shall take a party of women and fight for Guru-Sahib. We cannot sit by when innocent children are being bricked alive.' Fired by Mai Bhago's words, they started moving south towards the Lakhi Forest to join Guru-Sahib's forces.

Mai Bhago at Khidrana

On their way they learnt that Guru-Ji had come out of the forest and was camping at Khidrana. In those days this region was a complete desert and Khidrana had the only oasis which could provide water for a small force. They also heard that a large Mughal force from Sirhind was on its way to attack Guru-Sahib and decided to intercept it. Meanwhile, Mahan Singh and the band of deserters had been deeply shamed by Mai Bhago's words and taunts of women-folk of the region. They decided to try and make amends and re-join Guru-Sahib. As the Mughal forces reached that area, a fierce battle was fought at Khidrana in which Mai Bhago, dressed as a man, fought valiantly in the forefront. Mahan Singh and the deserters also fought, trying hard to atone for their earlier cowardice. Though greatly outnumbered, Mai Bhago inspired everyone with her heroism and the Khalsa forces prevailed. But all the forty deserters perished while fighting courageously.

After the battle, as Guru-Sahib went around the battlefield to comfort the wounded and dying, he found Mahan Singh mortally wounded. He propped him up in his arms and gave him some water to sip, telling him, 'I forgive you; go peacefully to your end.' Mahan Singh begged Guru-Sahib to destroy the paper of the forty traitors. Guru-Ji took out the paper and tore it up in front of Mahan Singh. Further, he told him that to honour their repentance and martyrdom, Khidrana would henceforth be known as Muktsar—the Oasis of Redemption.

Mai Bhago's companions too were all killed, while she was severely wounded. Guru applied a healing ointment and bandages to her wounds. She recovered completely and became a part of Guru-Ji's entourage, from where she continued to inspire Khalsa warriors till she breathed her last at Bidar (now in Karnataka).

32

An Eternal Guru

Unlike Akbar who had united the people by winning their hearts, Aurangzeb had kept his empire together by severe repression. As a result, rebellion after rebellion broke out and his Army was continuously involved in suppressing them. Aurangzeb had snatched the throne by killing his older brothers and imprisoning his aged and ailing father. Therefore, he was always suspicious that someone would do the same to him. Hence, he could not trust anyone in command of a big force—not even his sons. Thus, even in old age he was forced to go himself from one campaign to the next. As soon as he took the Imperial Army to fight in the south, the Rajputs would rise up in the west or Pathans in the north. He was fighting a rebellion in the Deccan when Bhai Daya Singh and Dharam Singh reached him with Guru-Ji's *zafarnama*. But due to the war, he could only meet Guru-Sahib's two emissaries some weeks after they had reached there.

The Emperor was shaken by the strong rebuke in the letter and his body started to tremble. He replied to Guru-Ji, explaining that he could not come to Punjab to meet him because of the fighting and requested Guru-Ji to meet him at Ahmednagar. He sent this reply through royal messengers. The Emperor's peace of mind had been shaken, he wrote to his sons that 'I do not know who I am, where I am and what will happen to a sinful person like me. Allah was in my heart but my blind eyes did not see him. ... I have committed many sins and do not know what punishments will be awarded to me'. He also gave instructions to his *Subedars* to withdraw all cases against Guru-Ji and directed that safe passage be ensured for Guru-Ji when he came to meet him.

Guru-Ji received Aurangzeb's reply while he was at Dam Damma. However, many Sikhs feared that this was a plot and Aurangzeb would harm Guru-Sahib. They advised him not to go. But Guru-Ji felt that if he was to put a stop to future atrocities against Sikhs and Hindus, he would have to take the risk. Also, he felt that the guilty people who had murdered his sons, broken their holy oath and committed even more offences, must be made to pay for their crimes. Since, only Aurangzeb could grant justice, he took the risk and left to meet him. He had reached only till Agra when he got news that Aurangzeb had died.

After Akbar, his successors had always fought among themselves to rule over the empire. Hence, the tradition of a peaceful and lawful succession had long been destroyed. Therefore, it was no surprise when Muazzam, the rightful heir, was attacked by his brothers and a war of succession broke out. All of them asked for help from Guru-Ji as well as from the *Subedars* and the Rajas. Choosing whom to support was a dangerous decision to make because, if one chose the losing Prince, then one's fate was sealed. But Guru-Ji at once decided to back Muazzam because as the eldest son, his succession to the throne was both legal and morally right.

After Muazzam had won the war of succession he became Emperor with the name of Bahadur Shah. He was immensely grateful to Guru-Ji and he conferred him with the title of *Hind ka Pir*; presented him with a robe of honour, prized Arab horses and other costly items. He also invited Guru-Ji for discussions and promised action against those guilty of crimes against Hindus, Sikhs and Guru-Sahib's own family. However, soon after the talks began, he had to leave for the Deccan where once again a rebellion had broken out. So, Bahadur Shah requested Guru-Sahib to accompany him and continue the parleys on the journey. Meanwhile, Wazir Khan of Sirhind was getting worried that Guru-Ji would be able to persuade the Emperor to make him answer for his crimes. So, he asked his supporters in the Court to somehow convince Bahadur Shah that helping Sikhs against his own Governor would not be good for stability of the Empire.

In a short time, Bahadur Shah had been convinced that he would suffer a lot of trouble if he took action against his own officers—even if that was the morally correct thing to do. So he let the talks drag on, saying that he was too busy with the battles against the rebels. Guru-Sahib accompanied Bahadur Shah till they reached Nasik by which time he sensed that Bahadur Shah had gone back on the promises made after he had won the war of succession with Khalsa help. So, he parted company from him and went on to Nanded.

At Nanded, Guru-Sahib met a *bairagi* (or hermit), Madho Das who had been born in Rajouri in the Jammu Hills area. He had impressed the local people with his magic powers and tried the same tricks on Guru-Ji. When they failed, he was stunned and at once realised that he was face to face with a very holy man. He fell at Guru-Ji's feet saying, 'I am your *banda* (slave)' and became his ardent disciple.

Soon after, General Saiyad Khan, who had become Guru-Ji's disciple and resigned from the Mughal Army, arrived from Kangra as he wanted to meet and be near to Guru-Sahib. However, one day he got a letter from his sister, who was *Pir* Budhu Shah's wife, that the Mughals had ransacked Sadhaura and hanged the *Pir* for being Guru Gobind Singh's follower. This meant that once again terror had been let loose on the people in Punjab. Guru-Ji at once started preparations to return to Punjab and bolster the spirits of the Sikhs.

Before he could leave Nanded however, two Muslim soldiers came to meet Guru-Sahib soon after the Reh Ras prayer. One of them, Wasil Beg, kept watch outside Guru-Ji's tent while Jamshed Khan stabbed him. Guru-Sahib immediately drew his kirpan and cut him down. The other was killed by the Sikhs as he tried to flee. The Sikhs suspected that Wazir Khan had hired them to kill Guru-Ji. When he got news of the attack, Bahadur Shah even sent his European surgeon to attend to him. But, though the doctor stitched up the wound, it opened again.

As he felt that his end was drawing near, Guru-Sahib announced in the *sangat* that there will be no living Guru after him and since the words of the Gurus were written down in the Granth Sahib, it would serve as the Sikhs' eternal Guru. On this occasion, he recited his own hymn:

'Agya bhayi Akal ki tabhi chalayo Panth
Sabh Sikhan ko hukam hai Guru manyo Granth
Guru Granth Ji manyo pargat Guran ki deh
Jo Prabhu ko milbo chahe, khoj shabad mein lay
Raj karega Khalsa aqui rahei na koye
Khwar hoe sabh milayngay, bache sharan jo hoe.'

The Khalsa Panth was created as directed by the Immortal One;

All Sikhs should now accept the Granth as their Guru since it contains the words of the living Gurus.

Those who seek God will find Him in the hymns of the Granth.

Only the Pure will reign and the impure shall be eliminated.

All devotees, including those who have been separated (from the Panth) shall achieve salvation.

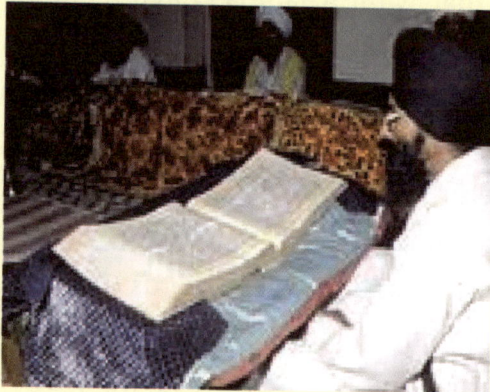

Guru Granth Sahib in Modern Times

The next day Guru-Sahib held a *durbar* and gave *amrit* to Banda Singh and announced, 'I appoint you, Banda Singh as my *jathedar* and give you the title Bahadur.' Then he took out five arrows from his own quiver and presented them to him. Next he handed him the Khalsa *Nishaan* saying, 'Go to Punjab and rid the land of tyrants; let all its citizens breathe the air of freedom; free from fear and terror.' He called five eminent Khalsas and appointed them as Banda Singh Bahadur's Council (*Hazuri Singhs*). Guru-Sahib also gave Banda Bahadur his own sword, bow and *nagara* (War drum). Finally, he handed over a Commission or *Hukamnaama* appointing him as the Sikh *Jathedar* and commanding all Sikhs to obey him.

As Banda Bahadur, with his five *Hazuri Singhs* and twenty-five soldiers, left Nanded on his mission, he was given a royal send-off by three hundred Sikh cavalry, who escorted the *Jathedar's* troop for a couple of *kos*.

Soon thereafter, Guru Gobind Singh Ji breathed his last.

ᗧ≈ᗤ ᗧ≈ᗤ

33

Banda Bahadur— The First Sikh Ruler

As directed by Guru Gobind Singh, Banda Bahadur came to the Punjab with his five *Hazuri Singhs* and twenty-five soldiers. He first eliminated a band of dacoits who used to rob and terrorise poor village-folk. This attracted many eager volunteers to his Army, which soon swelled to thousands. Samana, near present-day Patiala, was one of the first Mughal forts which he attacked and captured. This was also the home of the *shahi* executioners, brothers Bashal and Shashal Baig. The Sikhs captured and executed these two men, who had beheaded Guru Tegh Bahadur Ji as well as the two young *Sahibzadas*. After this, Banda Bahadur captured a string of Mughal forts in present-day Haryana and also destroyed many tyrannical Mughal landlords.

With the fall of each fort, the Khalsa Army was strengthened with a huge cache of weapons and horses. At the same time, the tax income from the area controlled by each fort brought in much-needed money to buy horses, weapons and to maintain the Army. On the other hand, Wazir Khan's revenues dropped rapidly and he was forced to personally come out and lead his forces to stop the Khalsa blitz.

The two armies met at Chapar Chiri near present-day Mohali. A fierce battle began between a huge Mughal force with thousands of war-elephants, cannon, cavalry and soldiers and the much smaller Khalsa Army consisting mostly of cavalry and foot-soldiers. But having drawn the main villain out of the fort of Sirhind to give battle in the open plain, Khalsa spirits were sky-high.

As the unequal battle raged, the *Jathedar's* call rang above the din of battle and was relayed from section to section. 'Wazir Khan must be taken alive. He must answer for his crimes!'

Electrified, the Khalsa forces surged forward with their war cry of '*Bolay so nihaal—Sat Sri Akaal*'. Though heavily outnumbered and facing the well-equipped, professional Imperial forces, their courage carried the day. Their only regret was that Wazir Khan could not be taken alive and was killed in the heat of battle.

Next, Banda Singh captured Sirhind and fulfilled his mission by utterly destroying the Mughal headquarters and ending all tyranny against Punjabis belonging to every religion. The remaining area in East Punjab soon fell to the Sikhs. Banda Bahadur Ji then found a natural fort in the hills at Mukhlispur, about ten *kos* north of Sadhaura. Here he established his capital and named it *Lohgarh*—the Steel Citadel. His official seal was in

Persian, which was the language of the Courts in those days. It read, '*Degh O Tegh O Fateh, nusrat-i-bedirang; yaft az Nanak Guru Gobind Singh*'. This means that, with hearts freed from narrow-mindedness by the *Degh's* magic, the Sword of righteousness (*Tegh*) has achieved victory (*Fateh*). The Rule of the Just has been created through the path shown by the ten Gurus from Guru Nanak to Guru Gobind Singh. He also minted the first coins of Sikh Rule in the name of Sacha Sahib (God) of Heaven and Earth.

Nowadays the words *Degh, Tegh, Fateh* form part of the *Ardaas*.

Banda Bahadur's Khalsa Coin

Thereafter, Khalsa forces captured the entire region of East Punjab up to the Yamuna, bordering Delhi. However, they took care to spare Maler Kotla, whose Nawab, Sher Khan, alone had the courage to oppose an imperial *Subedar*'s orders for executing the *sahibzadas*. Banda Bahadur very nearly succeeded in capturing Lahore and was only stopped at Shalimar Gardens, on its outskirts.

This alarmed Bahadur Shah, who visualised his kingdom being torn to pieces. He was forced to end his campaigns against rebels in the Deccan and also make to peace with the Rajputs and return with all possible speed to Delhi. Soon he amassed a huge Army which he personally led against Banda's forces. After many months of siege, the Sikhs were forced to abandon Lohgarh. Some years later, the Mughals succeeded in capturing Banda Bahadur whom they then executed in a most cruel manner. However, in spite of unspeakable tortures, all the captured Sikh men and women refused to change their faith.

During the very short period for which the First Sikh Commonwealth lasted, there was justice and freedom for all. Banda Singh Ji's administration also returned ownership of land to the Punjabi cultivators from whom it had been seized by Mughal conquerors and then destroyed the Mughal land records of *zamindars*. It took another three hundred years before this reform could be carried out in the rest of independent India. This may also be one reason for Punjab and Haryana becoming the top states in agriculture.

Mughal rule had been established by Babur who had generally followed Guru Nanak's advice to be a kind and just ruler. The Mughal Empire had grown and flourished. But Aurangzeb abandoned this policy and terrorised the Hindus. His tyrannical rule pushed the empire into a decline. The next emperor, Bahadur Shah, was persuaded to deny justice to Hindus and Sikhs as it might make enemies of some powerful people. Thus, Bahadur Shah lost all moral basis for ruling and his empire started crumbling.

34

Magic of the 'Degh' in Modern Times

Traditions established by the ten Gurus and the *degh's* magic continue to cast their spell in modern times. Here are three examples.

1. A Ferocious Storm

On 29th October 1999 a ferocious super-cyclone hit Orissa on India's east coast. The storm was so terrifying that people fled in panic from their homes. The raging storm ravaged half the State and completely cut-off the whole region. This is one disaster this author personally experienced as we rushed with the Indian Army to help the stricken people. Fifteen million had become homeless and more than ten thousand died in the storm. The State capital, Bhubaneshwar was totally paralysed and people were starving as the Army raced to get the relief camps up and running. After a few days the author was able to visit the Patnaiks, his friends in Bhubaneshwar, to see if they needed any help.

'You Sikhs are truly amazing,' Patnaik said, 'the gurudwara in Cuttack (this is just across the river

Guru-ka-langar in Orissa

from the capital city) has opened *Guru-ka-langar* here in Bhubaneshwar and it is feeding thousands and thousands of people. Their own homes are just as badly hit as ours; still they have found the will to help out this city. What is more marvellous is that when even the Government cannot get rice and other food-stuff, the Sikh *langar* somehow keeps running day and night.'

Actually, people in Punjab had donated generously and volunteers had loaded hundreds of trucks every day and sent all this relief as gifts to Orissa. Thus the spirit of *sewa* continues to give joy to those who serve and love their fellow human beings.

2. Sewa During Mumbai's 26/11 Terror Strike

On 26th November 2008, terrorists attacked a number of places in Mumbai. They took control of two world-famous hotels and held all the guests hostage. Army commandos of NSG were flown in and began a powerful counter-assault to defeat the terrorists and free the hostages. As fierce fighting broke-out, terrified people

Taj Hotel, Mumbai on 26 November 2008

fled from the area. The Army Commandos had been rushed in such a great hurry that the Mumbai Police did not have time to make food arrangements for them.

However, young Sikhs of gurudwara Dashmesh Sahib, Sion, ignoring flying bullets and bursting grenades, established a *Guru-ka-langar* next to the fighting. From here they provided hot food, day and night to the soldiers as well as to all needy people—all *Akaal Purakh's* children. They also helped in evacuating those who had been wounded and injured in the fighting.

3. A Green Hero for our Times

Baba Balbir Singh Seechewal, a Sikh holy man in Punjab was horrified to find that the Kali Bein, the river where Guru Nanak had gained enlightenment, had now become a stinking drain, choked with weeds, refuse and filth. He made a quick trip along the river to find out the causes and then decided to do something about it.

'This is the river in which Guru Nanak used to bathe every day.' he told people in each gurudwara of the area. 'Its waters were so clean and fresh that he gained enlightenment here. Now see how it has become a drain and all of us are falling sick because it is so filthy.'

The Sikhs living nearby realised the truth of his words. 'Come on,' he said, 'let's clean up this mess and make the river as pure as it was in Guru Nanak's time.'

Kar-sewaks cleaning the Bein River

Thousands of *kar-sewaks* (volunteers) responded to his call, taking control of their own lives and environment instead of waiting endlessly for Government to act. They cleared the entire riverbed of water hyacinth and silt and built roads along its banks. Then they stopped industries from pouring untreated pollution and sewage into the river. Now, once again, the river-water is sparkling, it has become a picnic spot and health-hazards in the area have disappeared. Devotees can bathe in its crystal water during religious festivals. After this success, the Baba inspired the people and government to clean up more rivers.

Baba Seechewal and the sparkling Bein

In September 2008, Time magazine of USA declared Baba Balbir Singh Seechewal one of the planet's 30 Environment Heroes.

Motivated by Baba Ji, all gurudwaras have started giving *prasad* of saplings (*buta-prasad*) to devotees as part of the *Nanhi Chhaan* Project (literally—baby shade). While planting trees helps save the environment; the project reminds everyone that girls and boys are equal and just as precious. *Nanhi Chhaan* Project has now become a National Foundation and is including more states and temples such as *Vaishno Devi* temple near Jammu, the Garibh-Niwaj Dargah at Ajmer and Sacred Heart Cathedral, New Delhi.

As we combat global warming, Baba Seechewal is getting the world's religious leaders together to enlist their help in the struggle to save the planet. A Sikh Eco plan has also been inspired by the Baba.

The magic of the *degh* continues to inspire *sewa* and charity for meeting challenges now facing planet earth and to break down barriers between human beings—artificial barriers of caste, creed, colour and sex.

☜☞